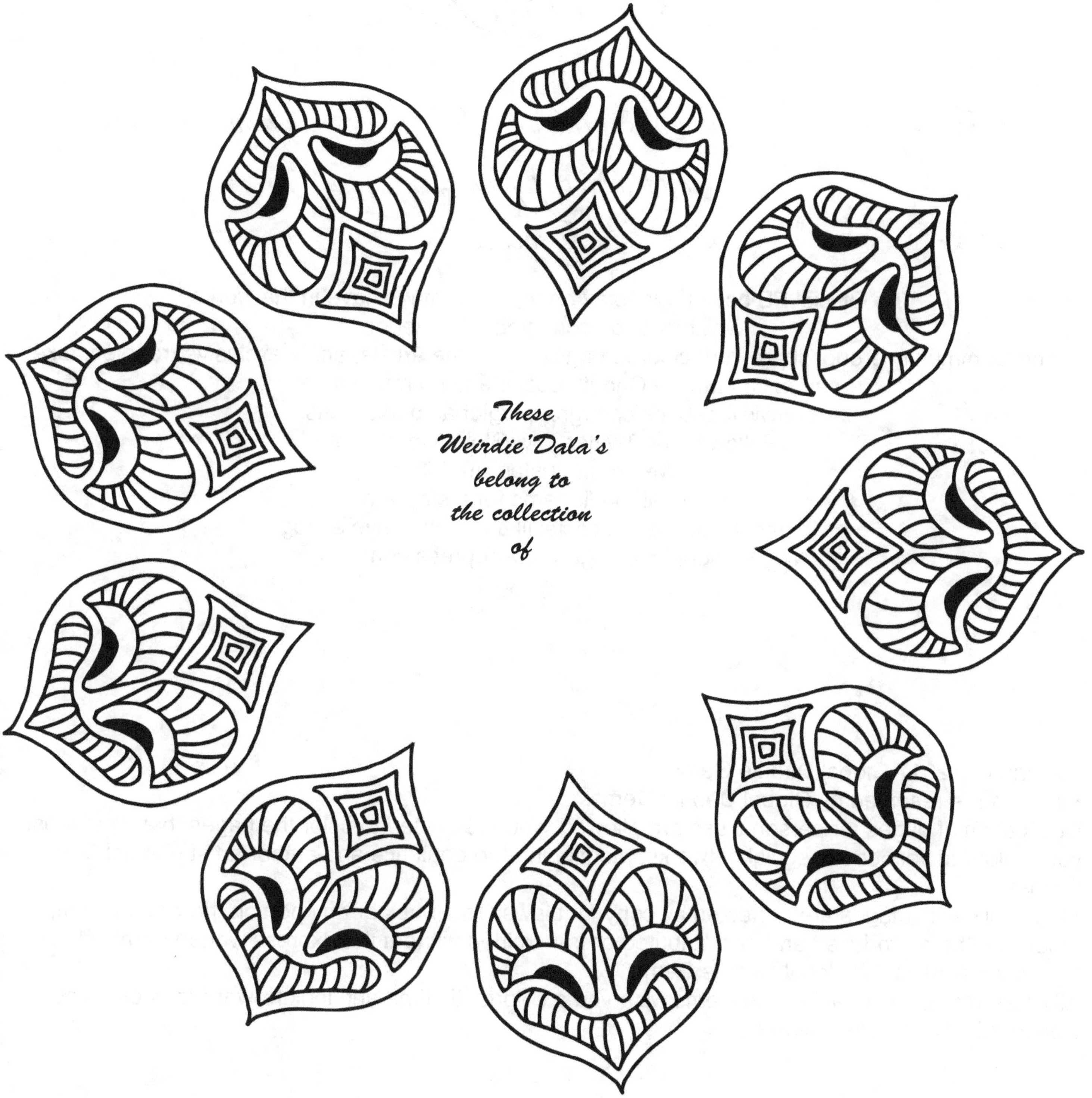

These
Weirdie'Dala's
belong to
the collection
of

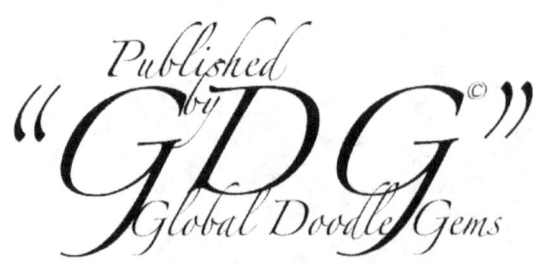

Share your colored versions with us ! We love seeing your results and hearing from you we are social !

The Official FB book page, stay on top of what we have in the works !
www.facebook.com/globaldoodlegems
The Community group, share your colored pages, meet the artists, enjoy exclusive freebies, take part in community Charity books and so much more......
www.facebook.com/groups/globaldoodlegems/
Follow us on Twitter.... @GlobalDoodlegem
We are on Instagram too
@globaldoodlegems for instagram
...and if you are not social like that we have a blog
globaldoodlegems.wordpress.com

Copyright © 2017 Global Doodle Gems
All rights are reserved by Global Doodle Gems.
Duplication of pages for personal use are allowed. You are invited to color the pages then scan/post your coloured versions to social networks, mentioning the book title and author/artist (Global Doodle Gems).
All artwork and images are protected by copyright laws. This book or any portion thereof may not, otherwise, be reproduced and/or distributed or transmitted without the express written permission of the artist/publisher of Global Doodle Gems.
All of us from the Global Doodle Gems wish you a colortastic time and look forward to seeing your wonderful color results online !

Welcome to my world of Weirdies

This series of drawings are dedicated to all the weird, whimsical,
wacky and totally amazing people in the world !
Through art and coloring I have met and befriended
so many amazing personalities,
and come to discover just how awesome,
incredible and giving strangers can be,
and how fast a stranger can become a dearly loved
friend, through the coloring world I have met
amazing artists and stunning colorists,
I have been overwhelmed and delighted by this
amazing journey of discovery and
discovering new corners of my imagination and art,
the 'Weirdie'Dala's is a part of a Weirdie a day series !
I will make 12 books, one for each month of the year, with
a Weirdie for each day, in addition I have made the Weirdie'Dala's, the
Weirdie version of Mandala's, to have a fun time with !
Sending out a huge embrace to all of you !

Maria Wedel

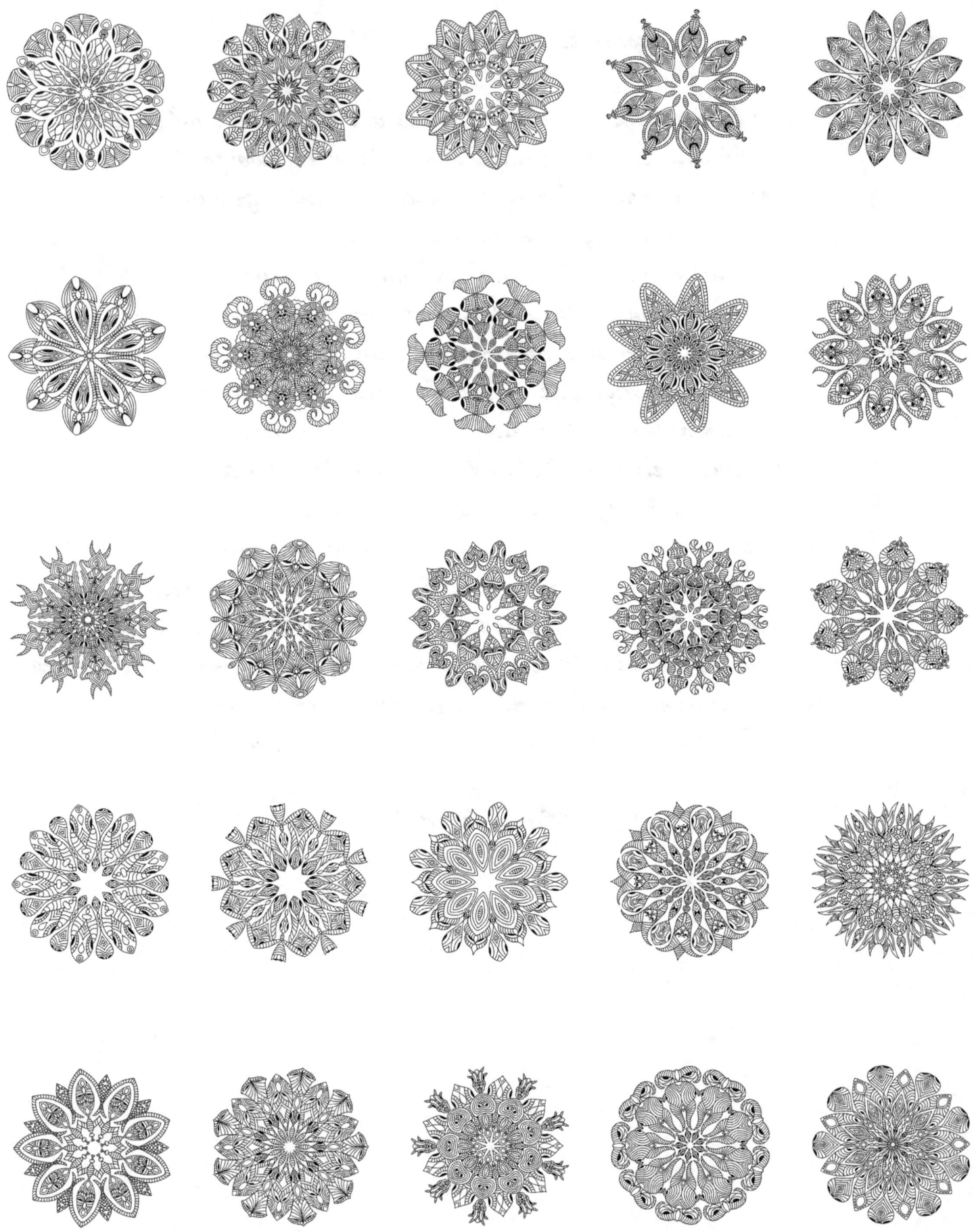

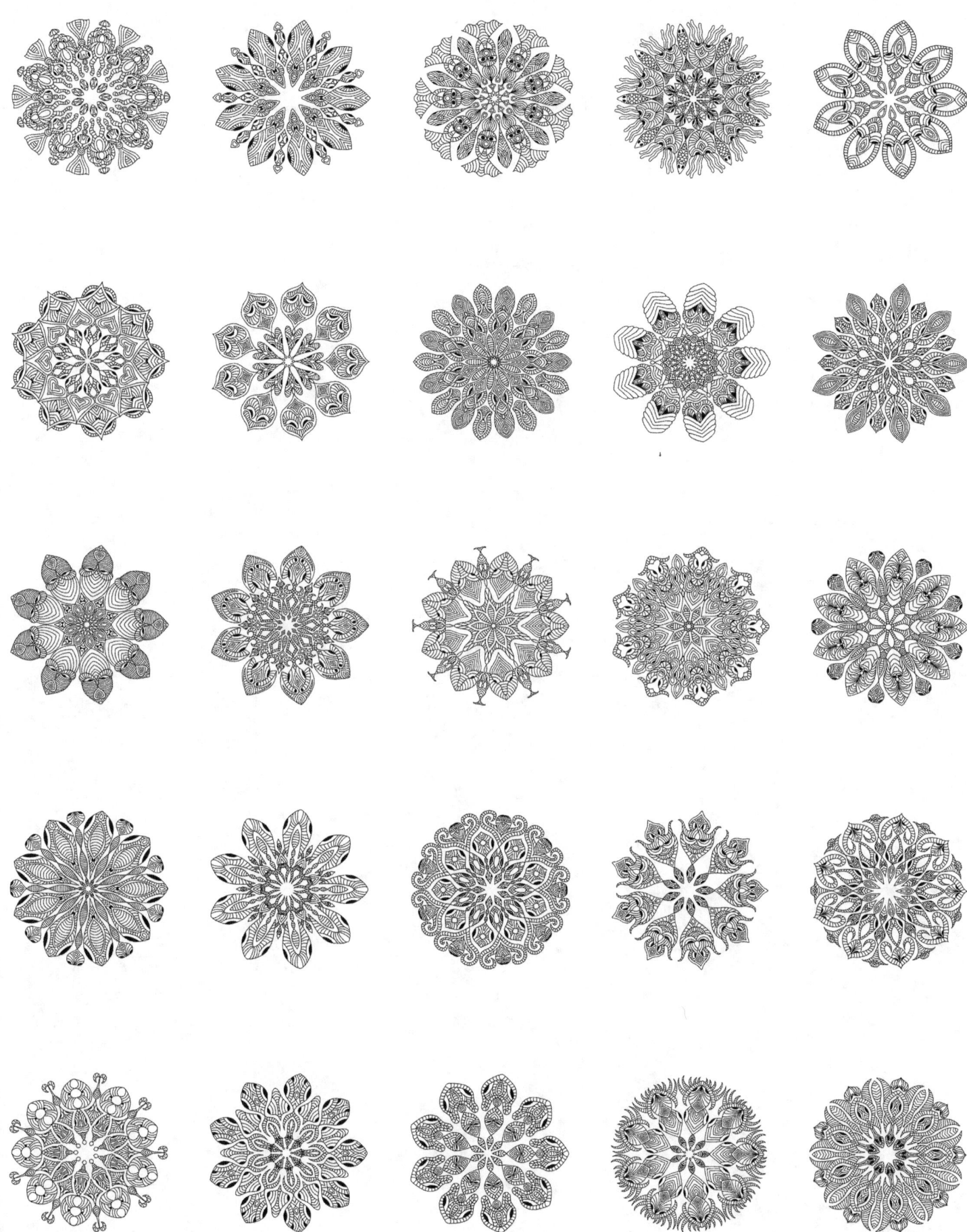

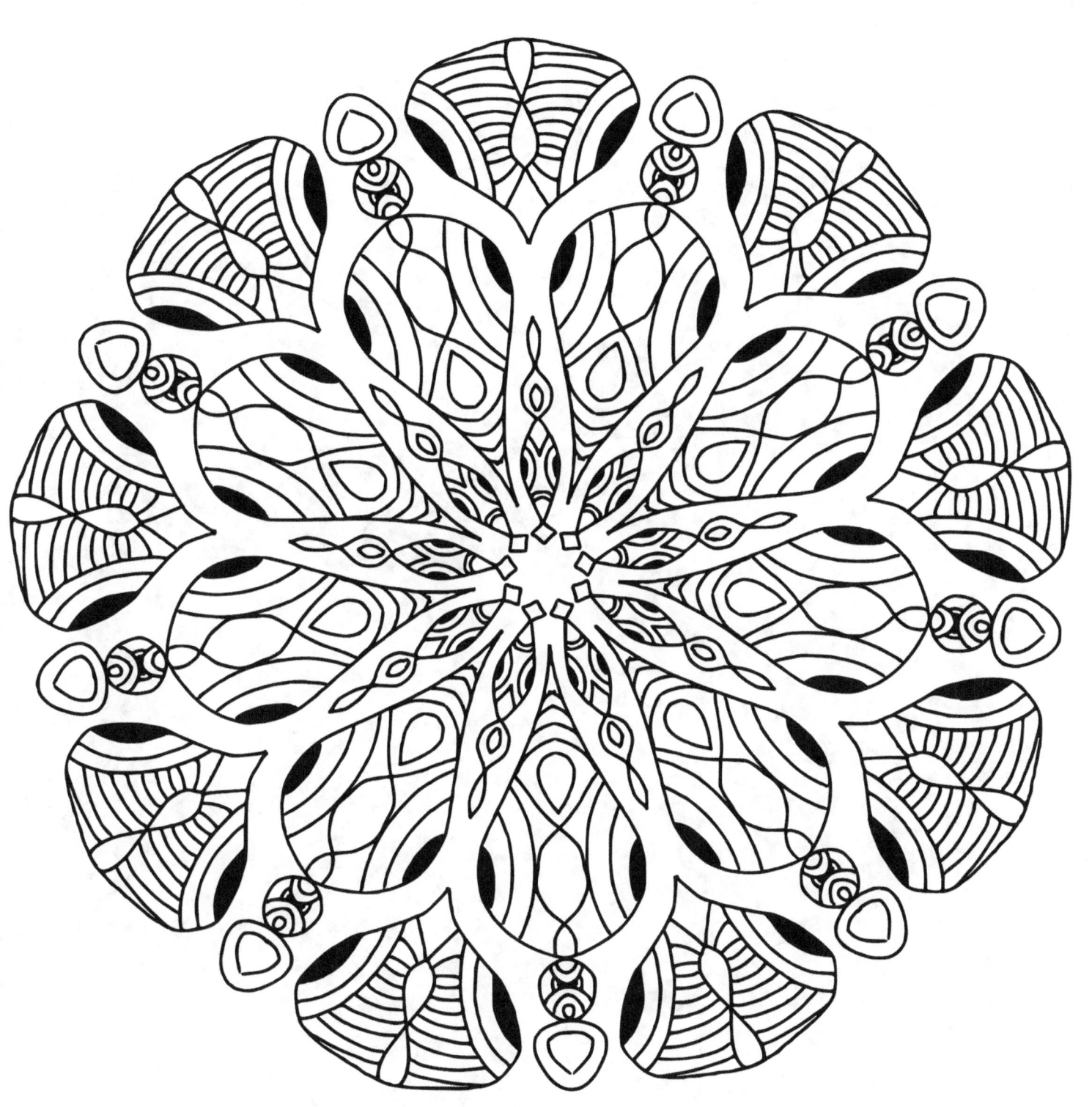

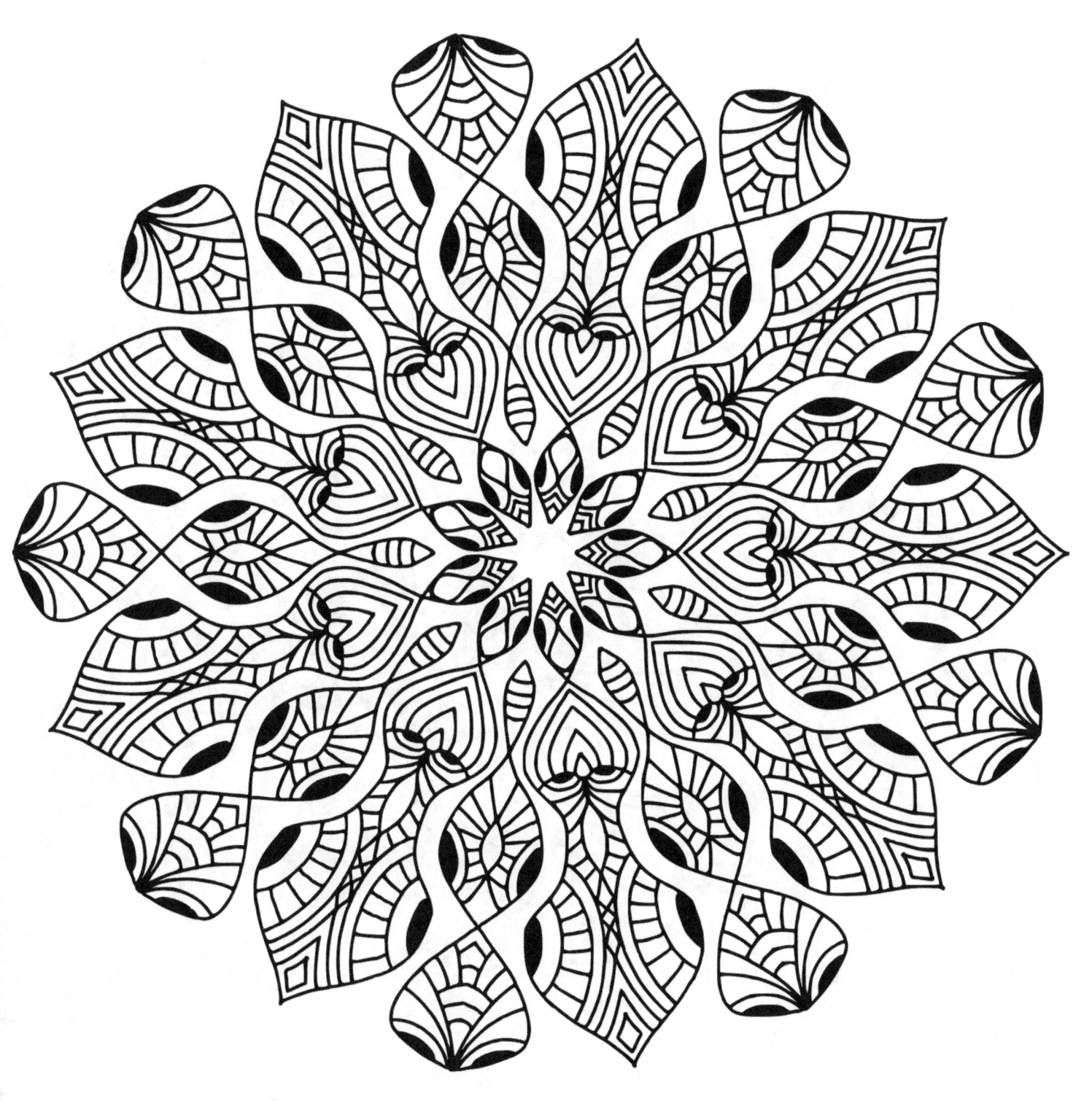

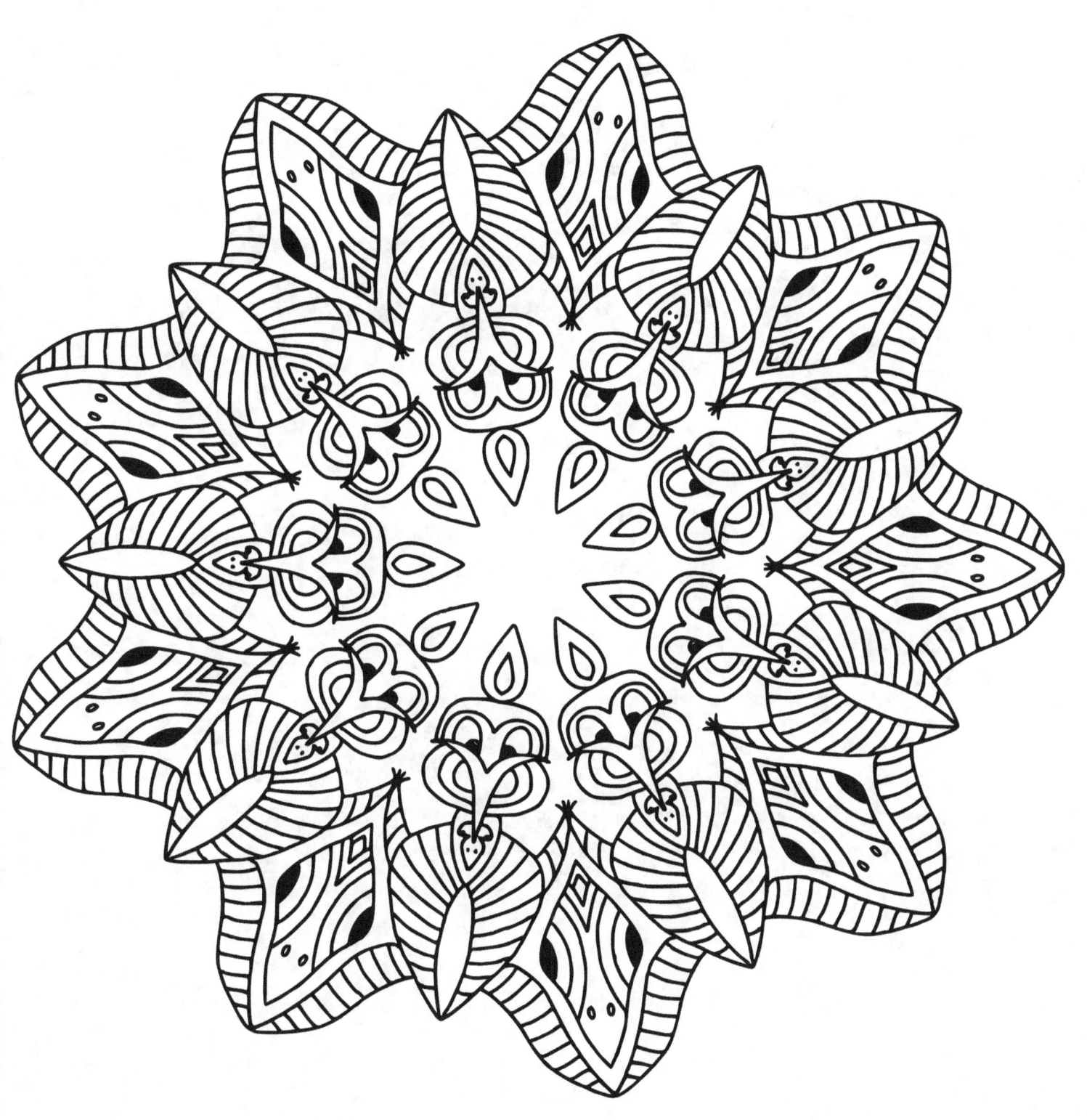

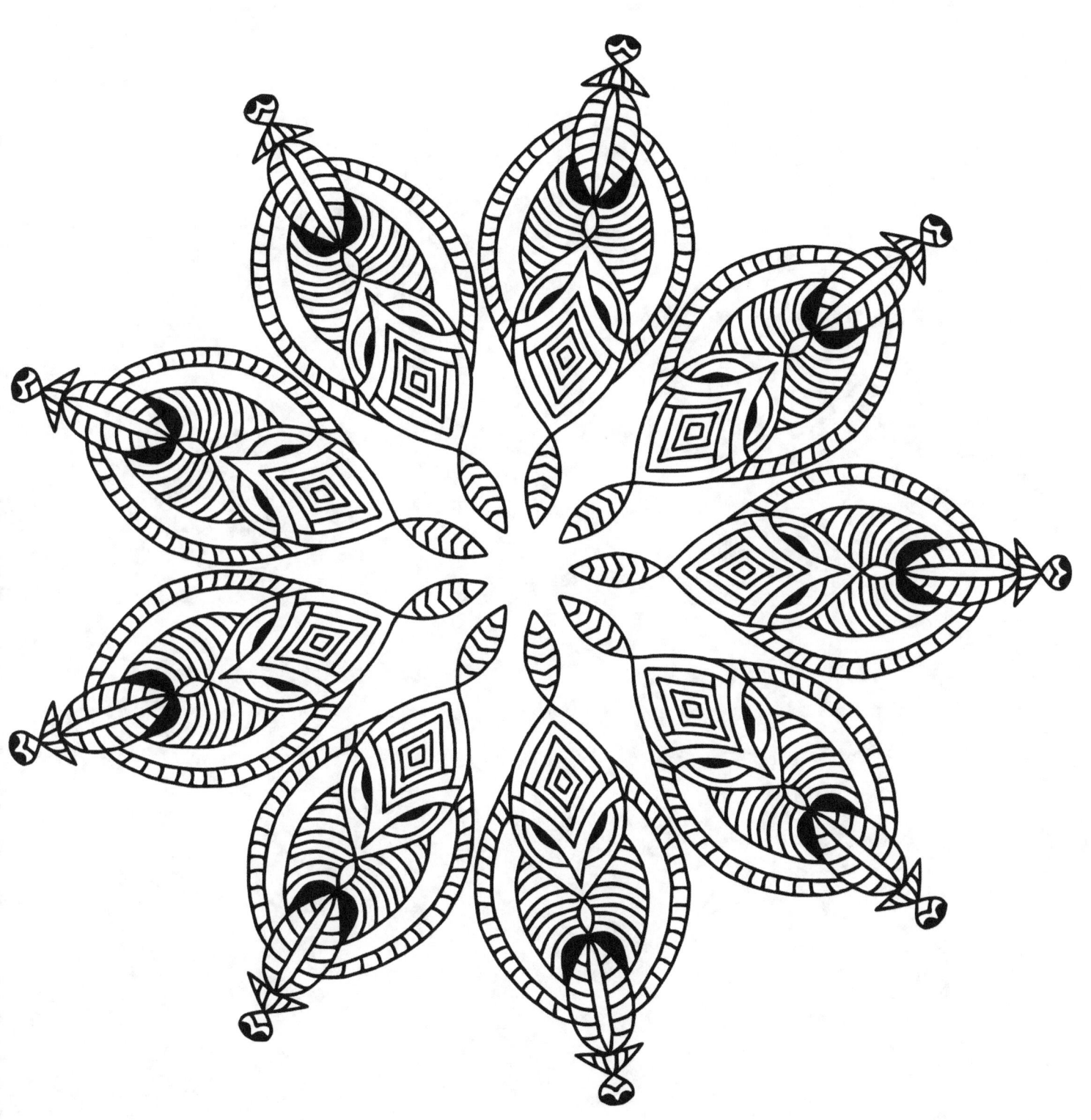

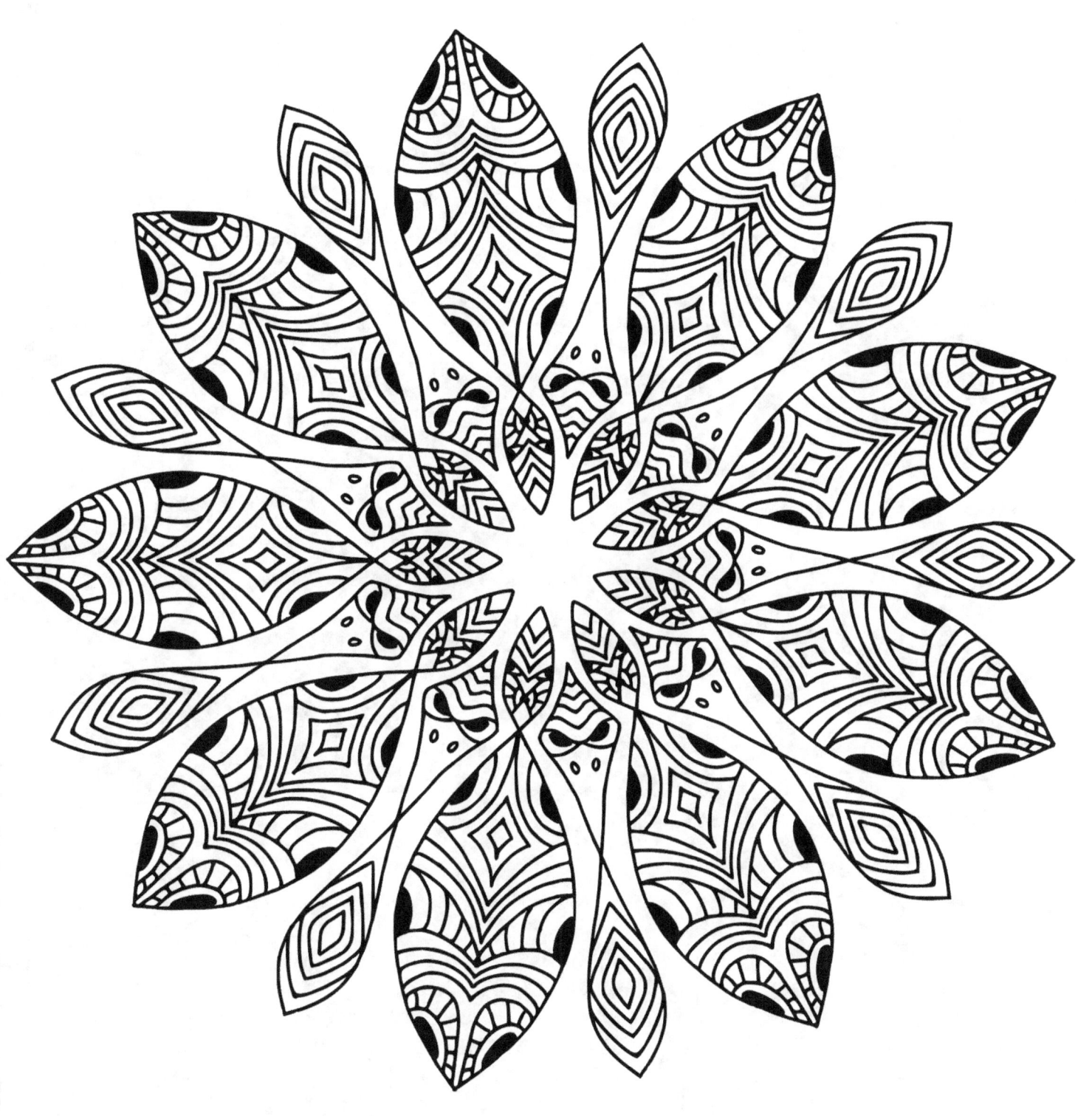

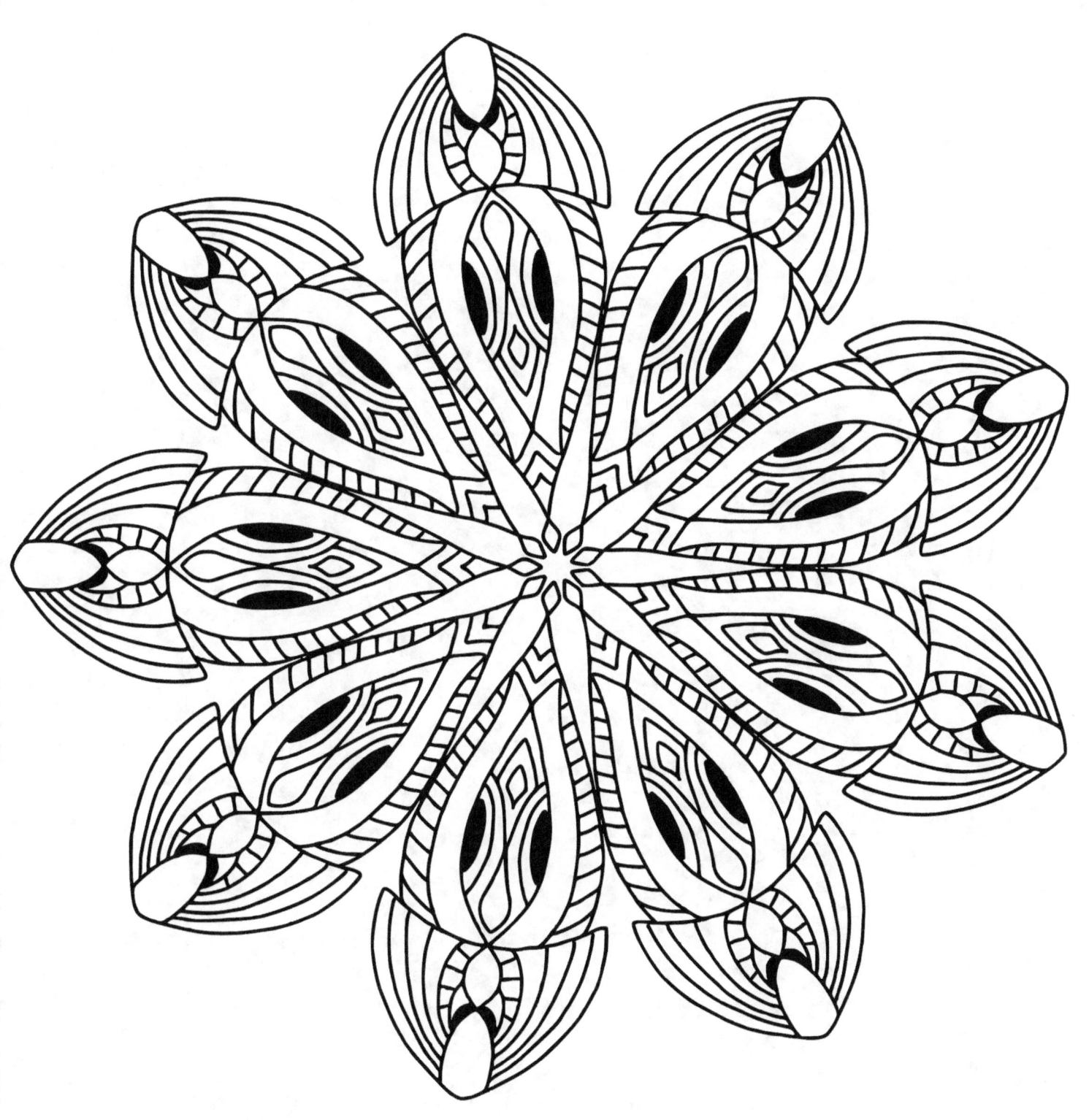

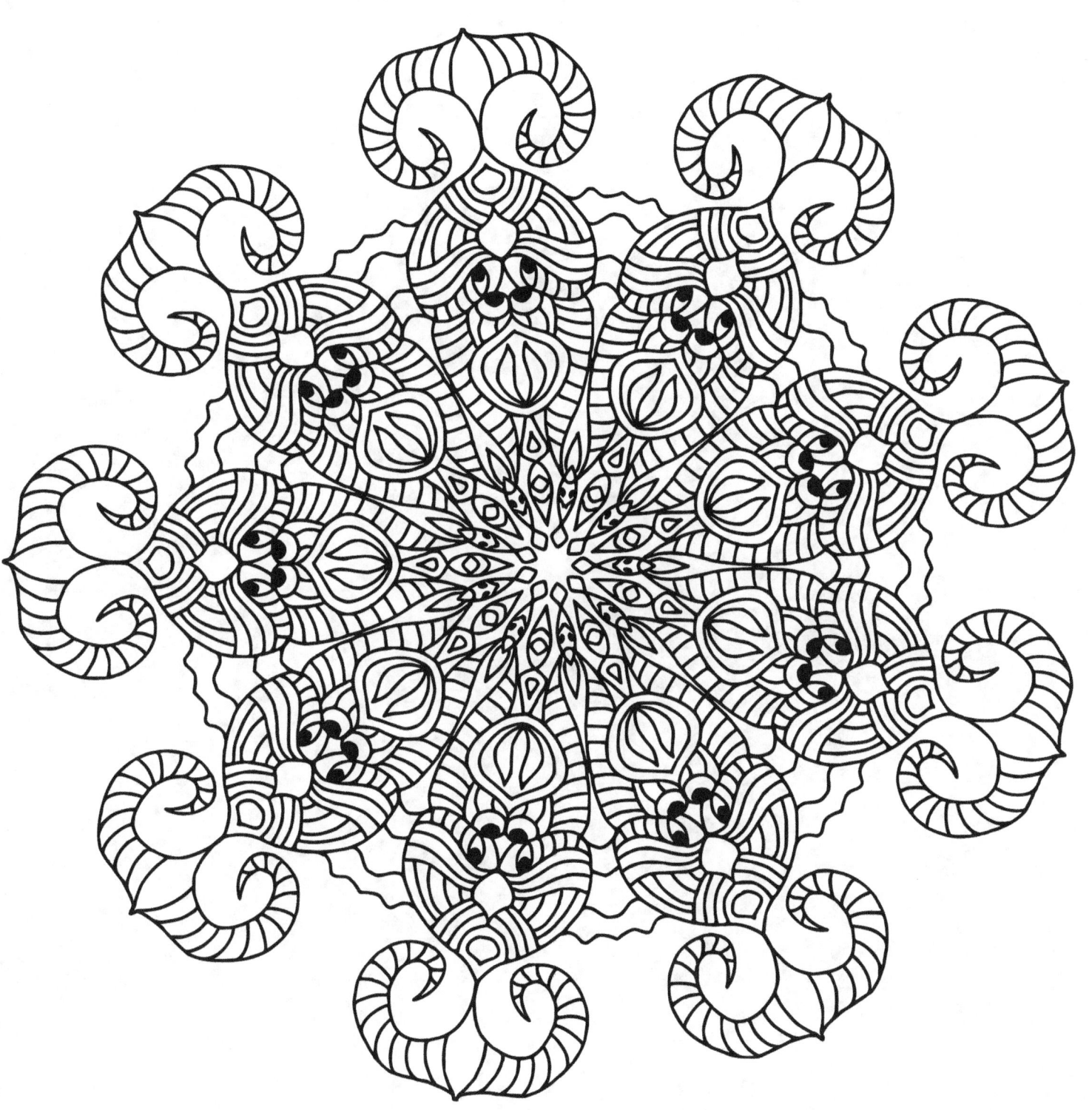

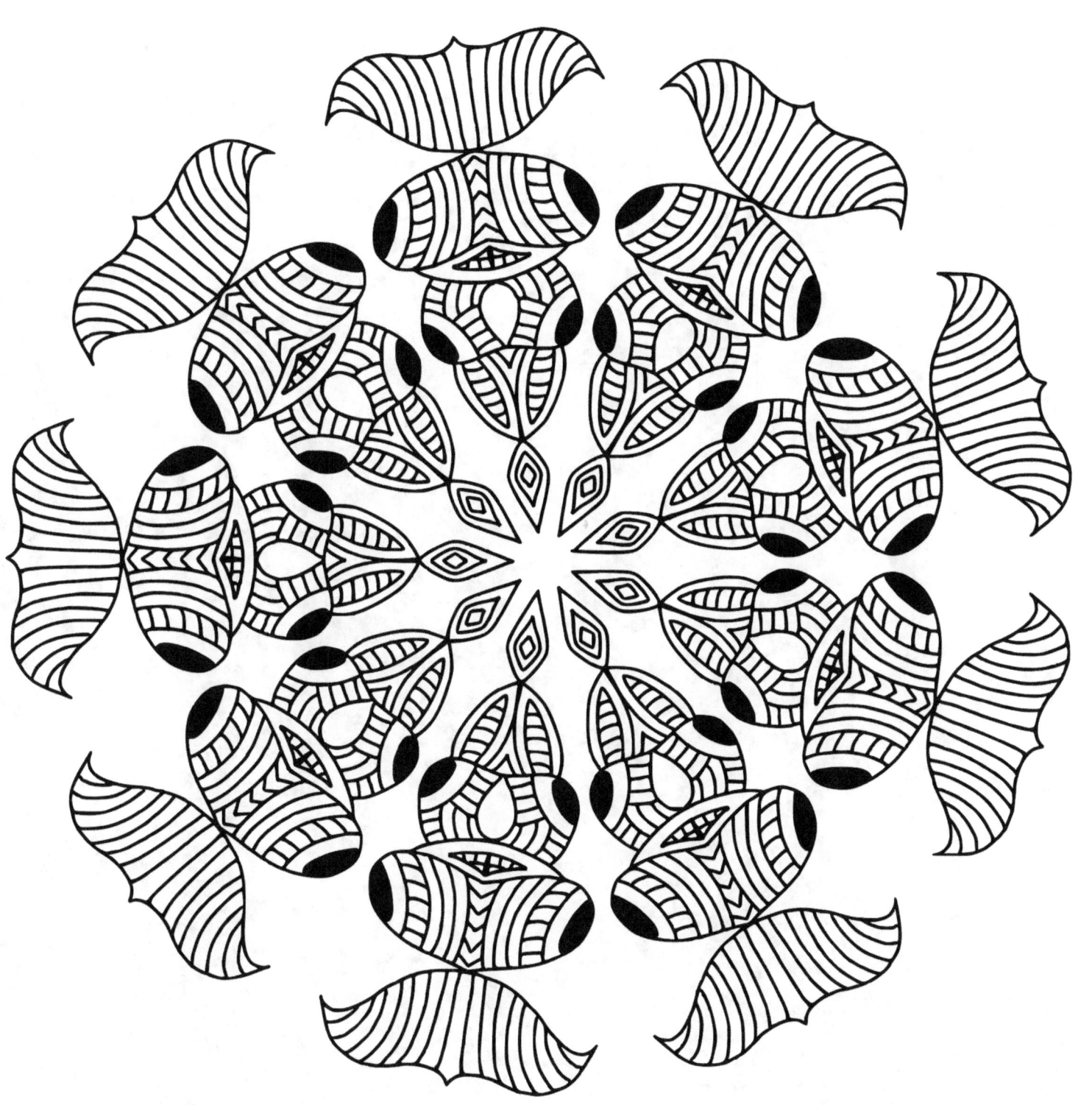

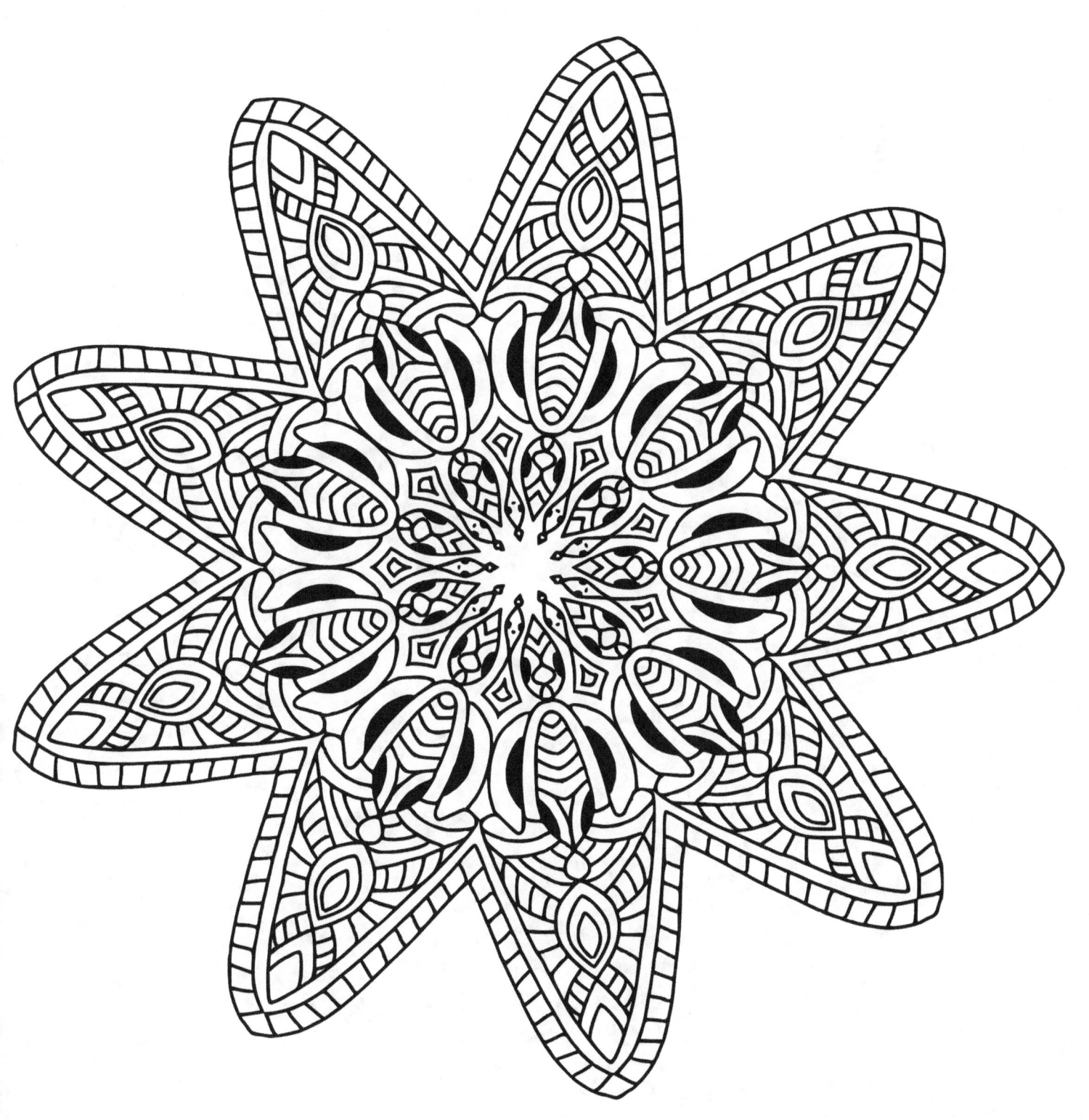

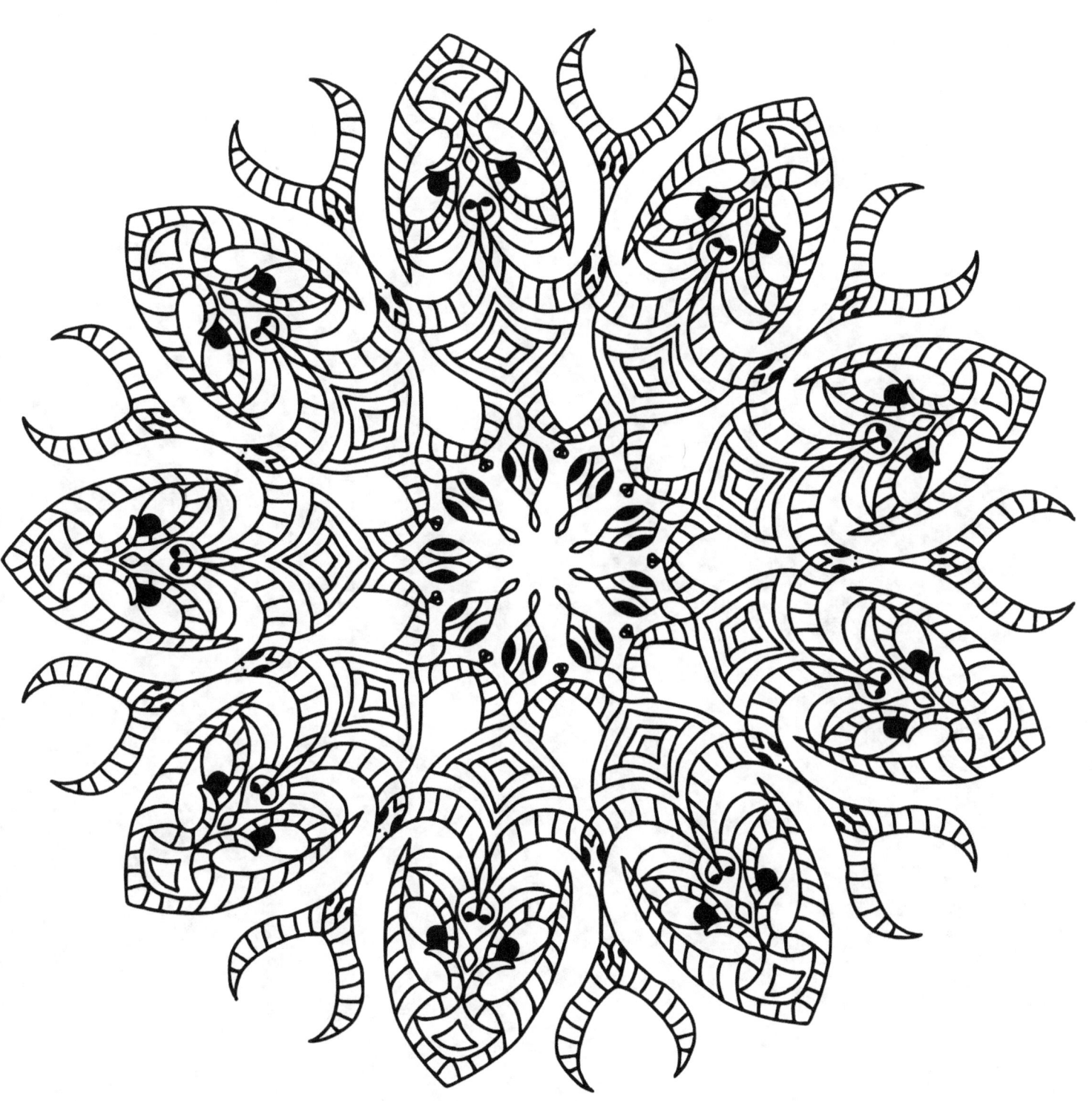

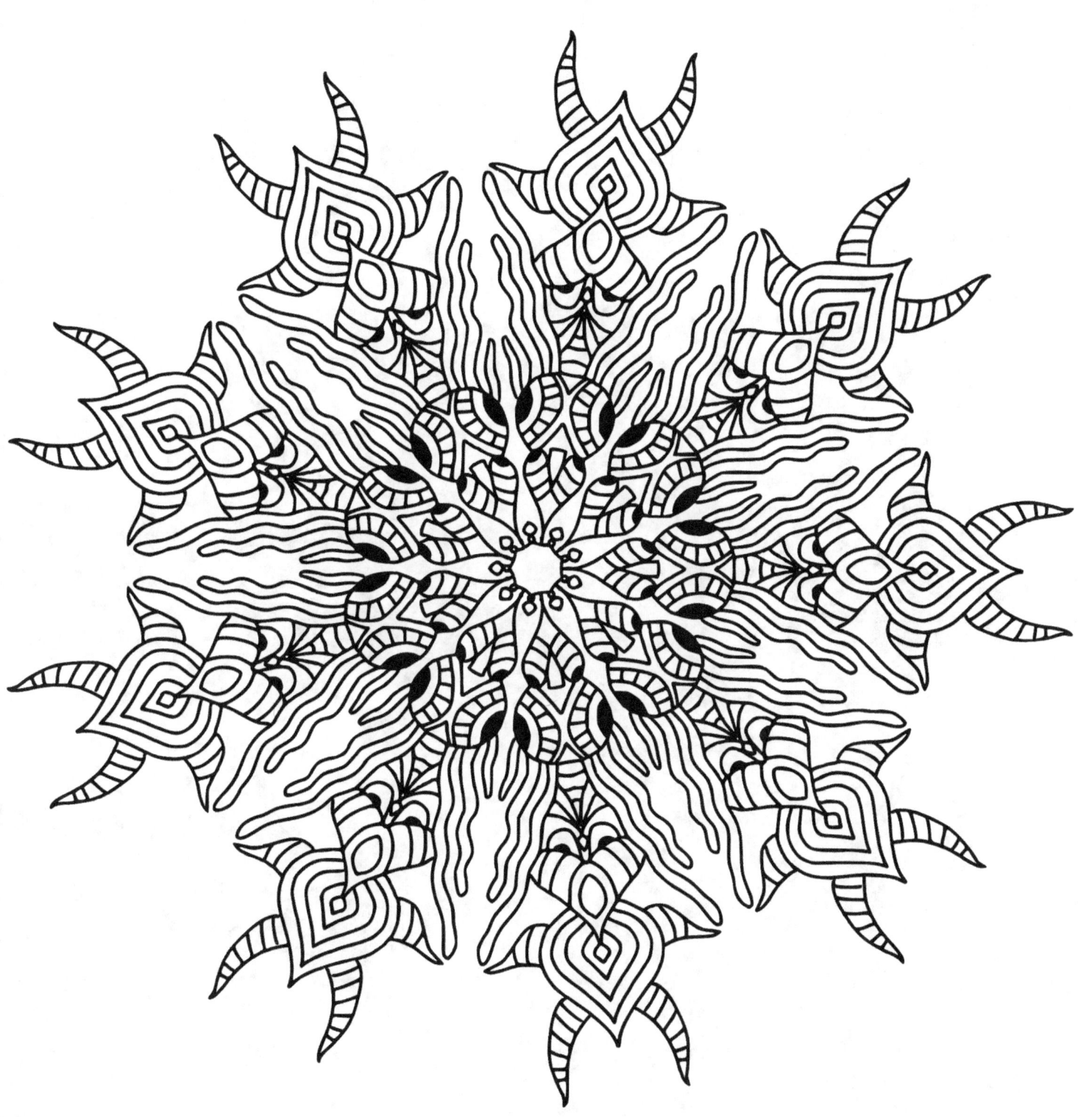

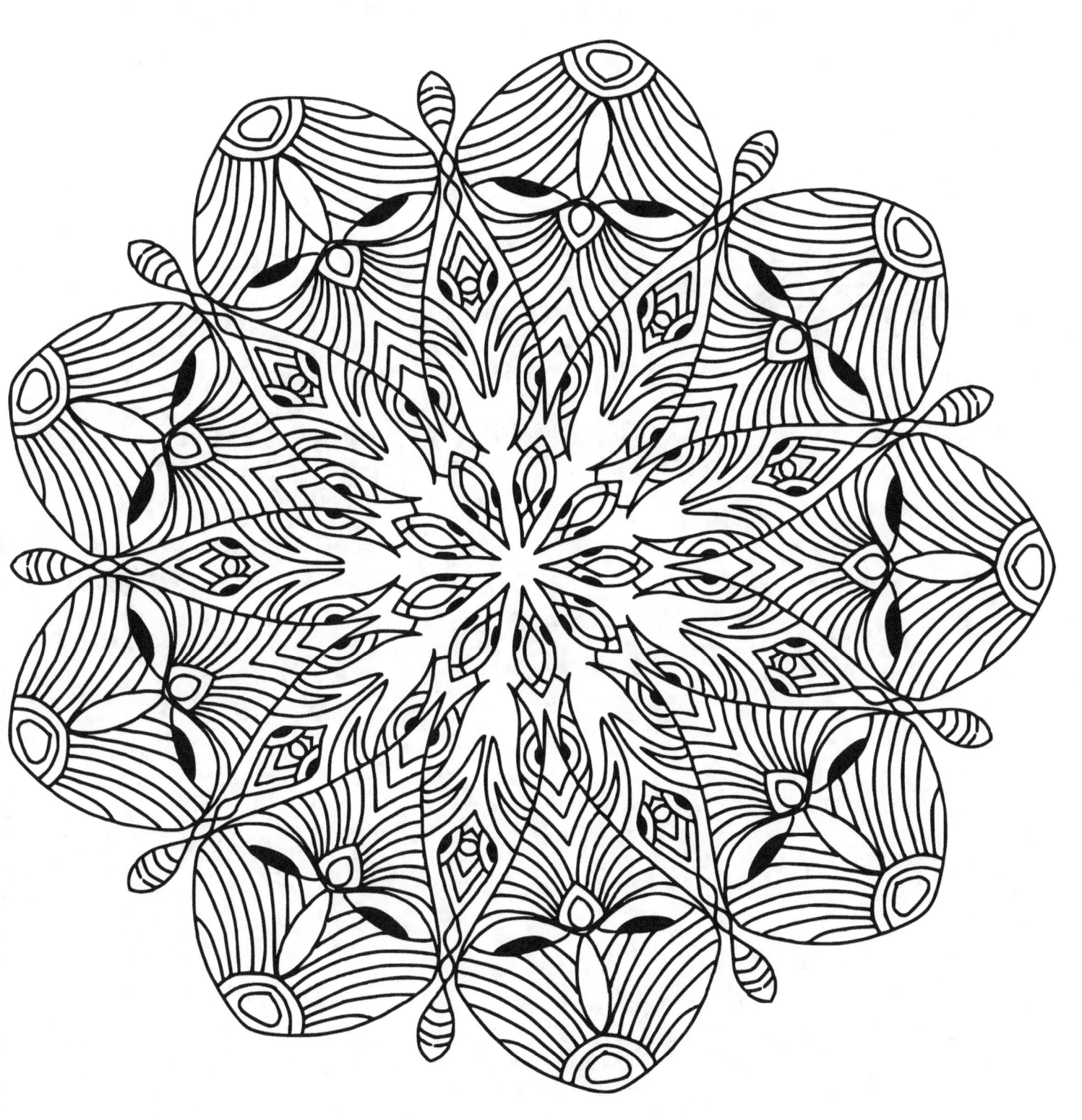

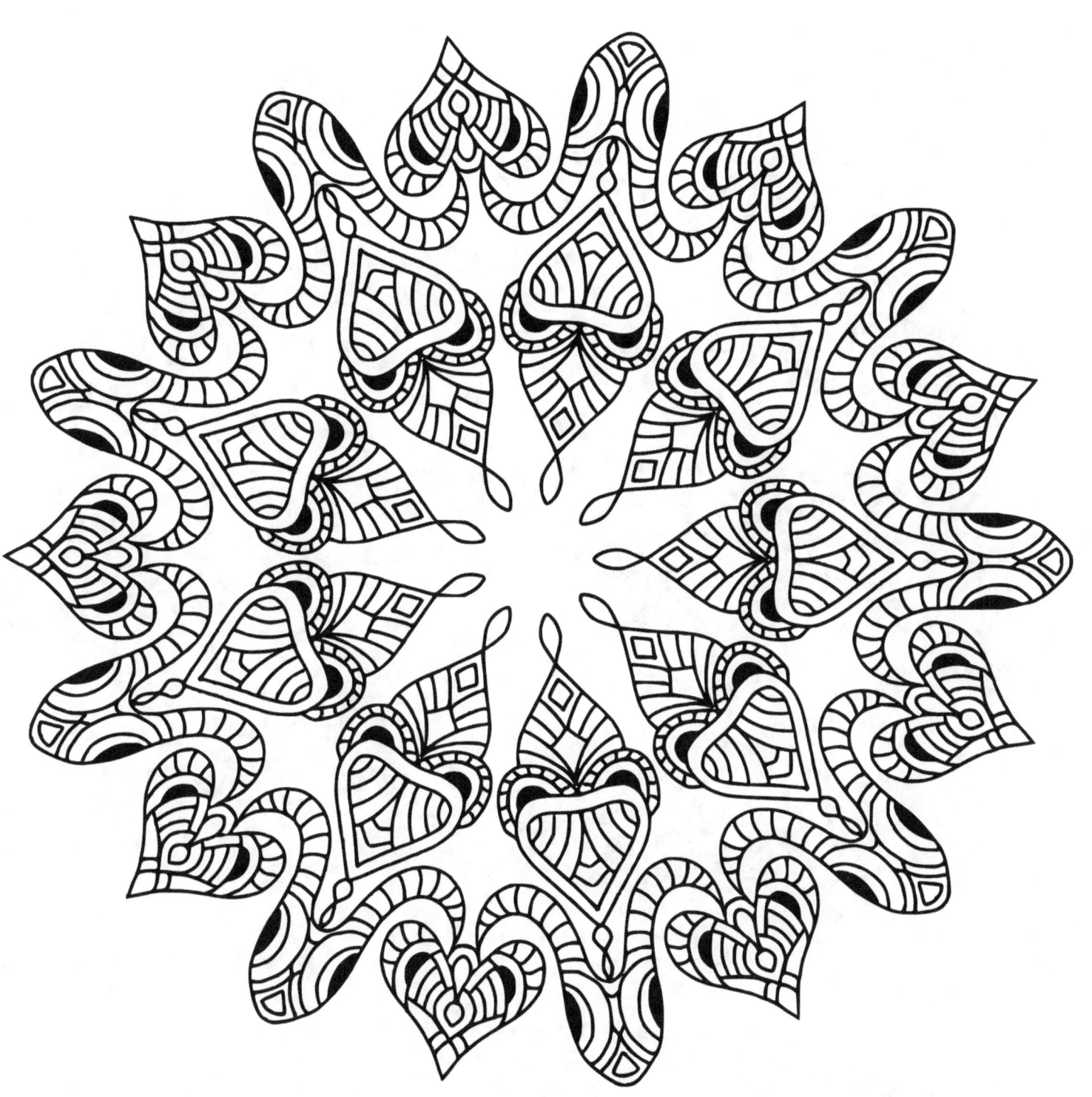

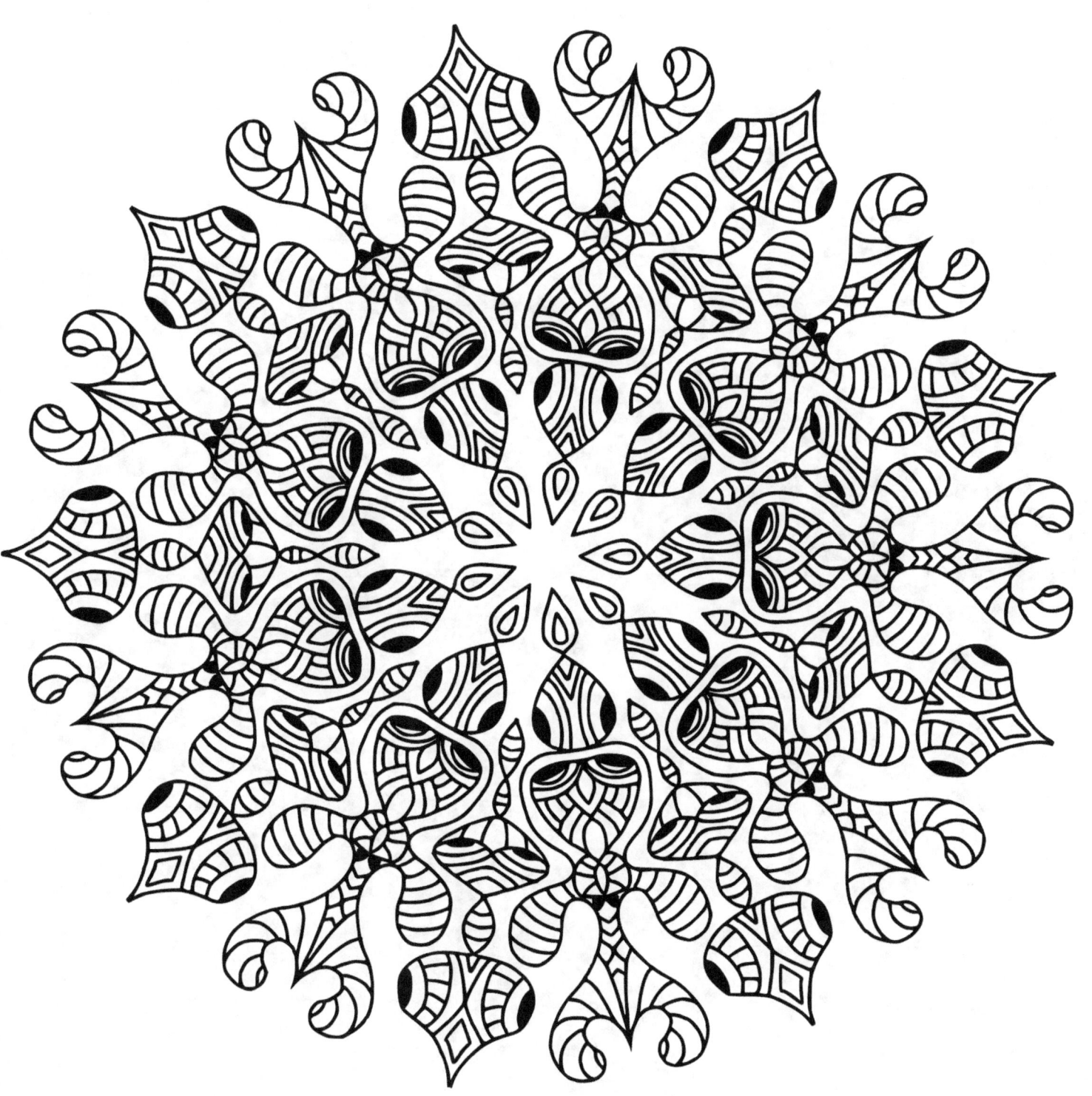

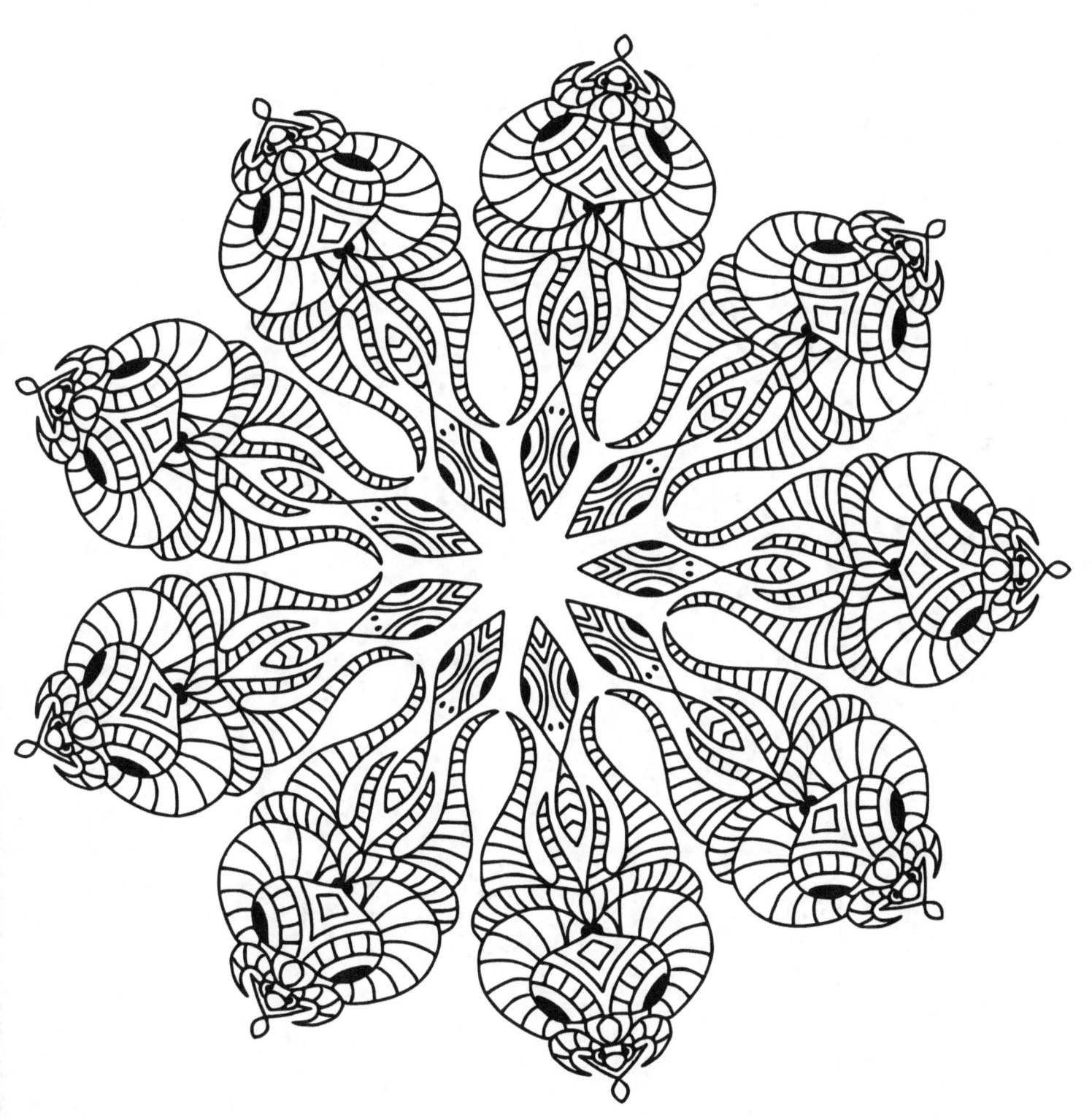

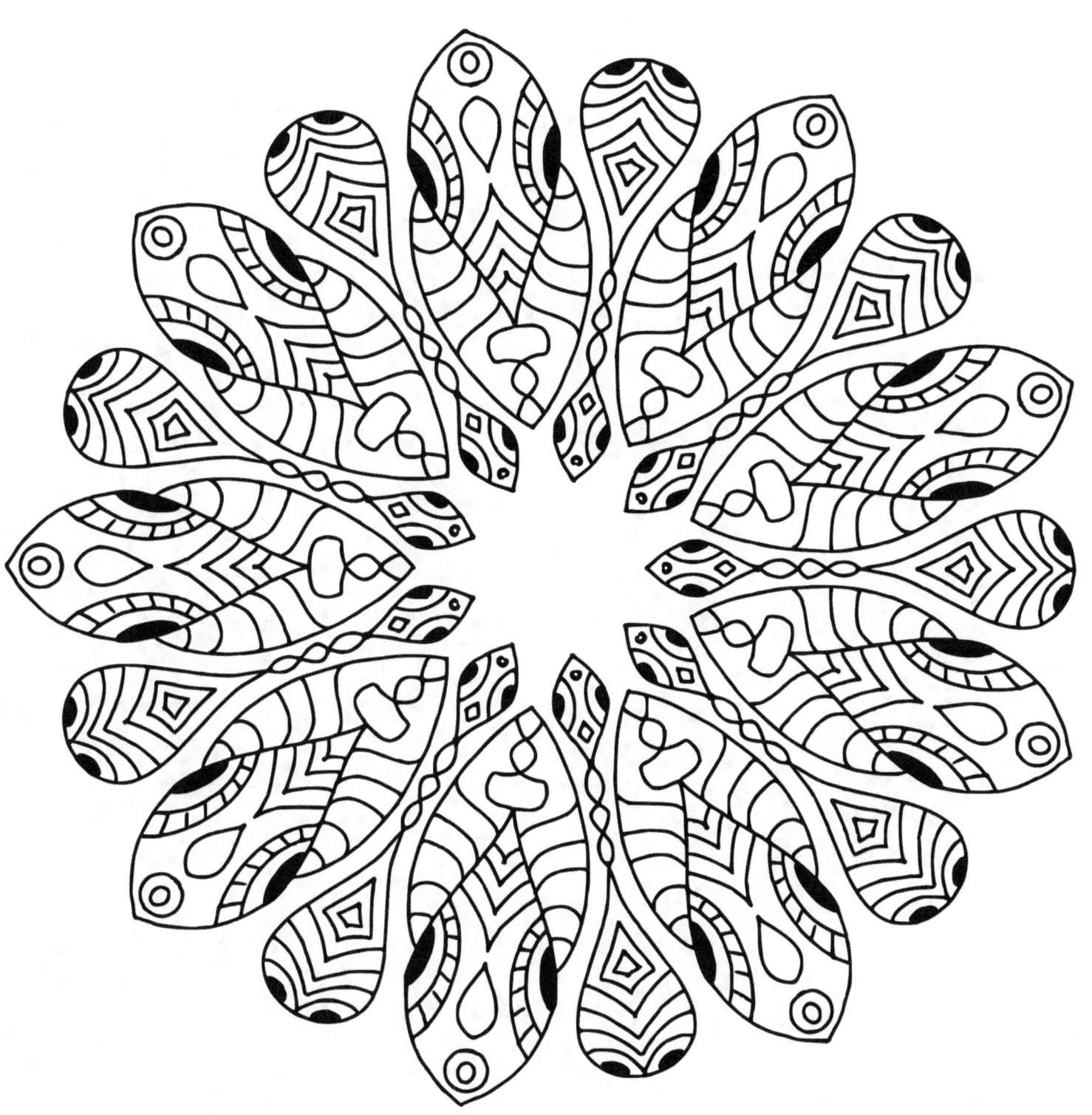

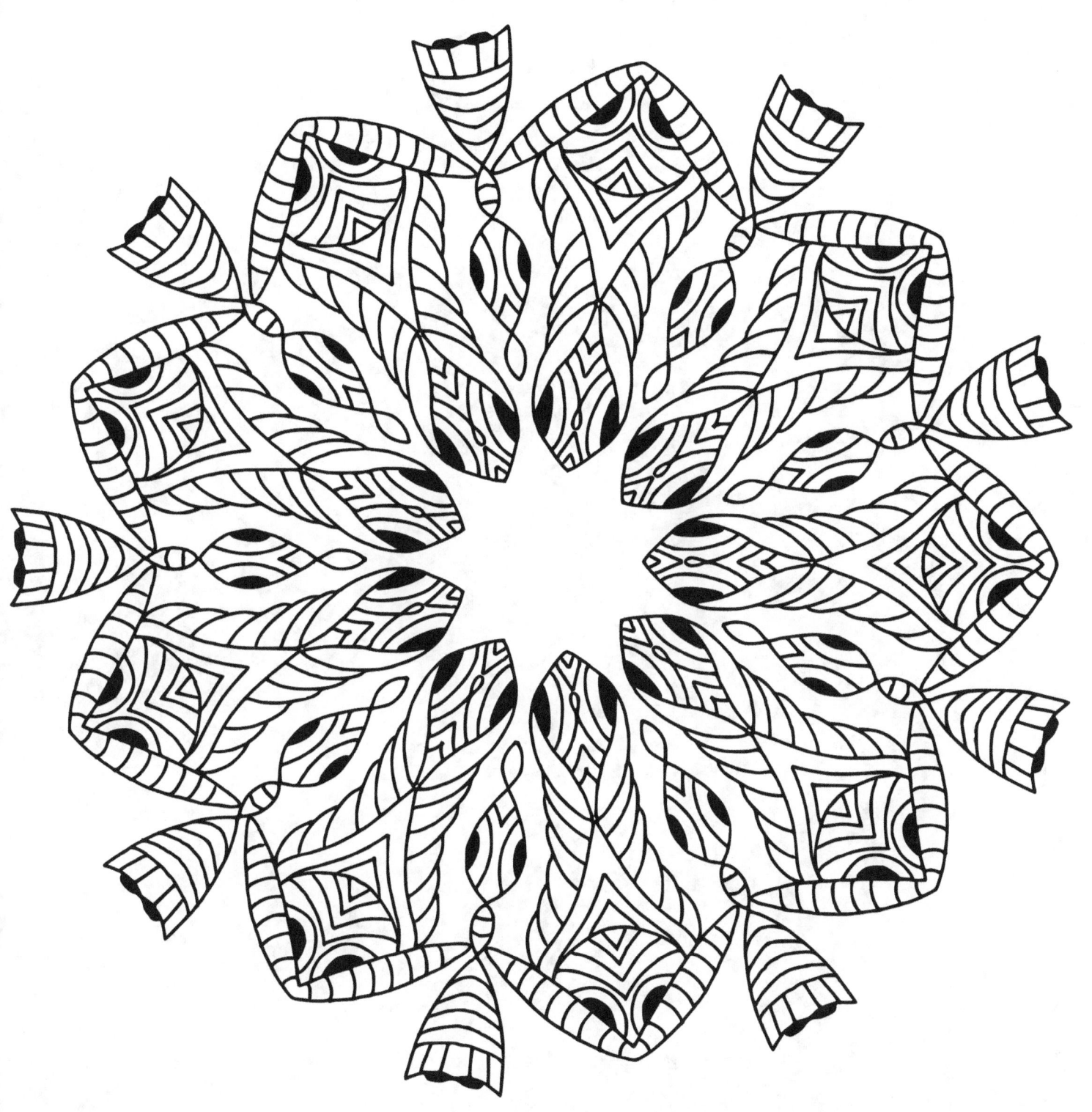

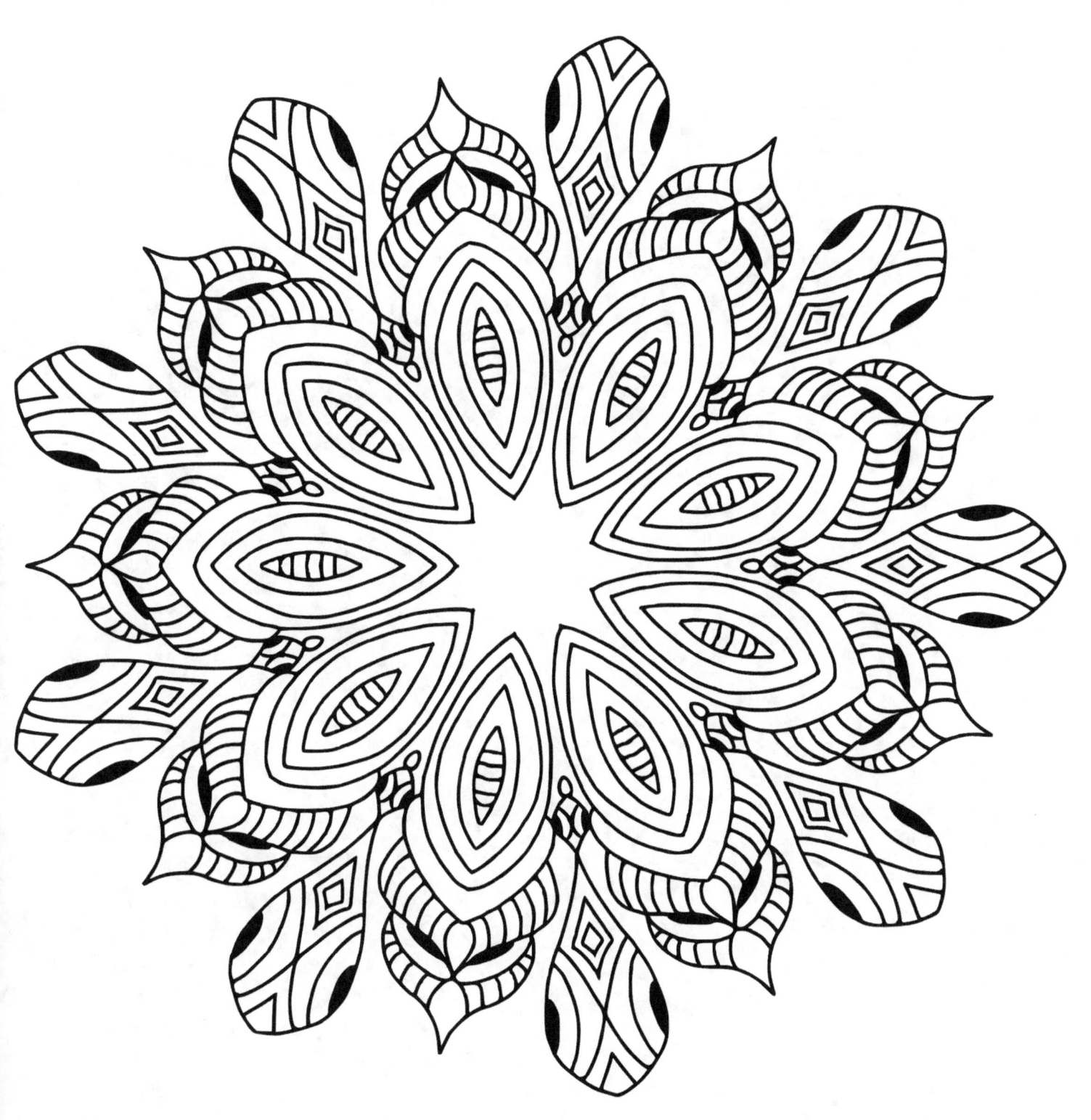

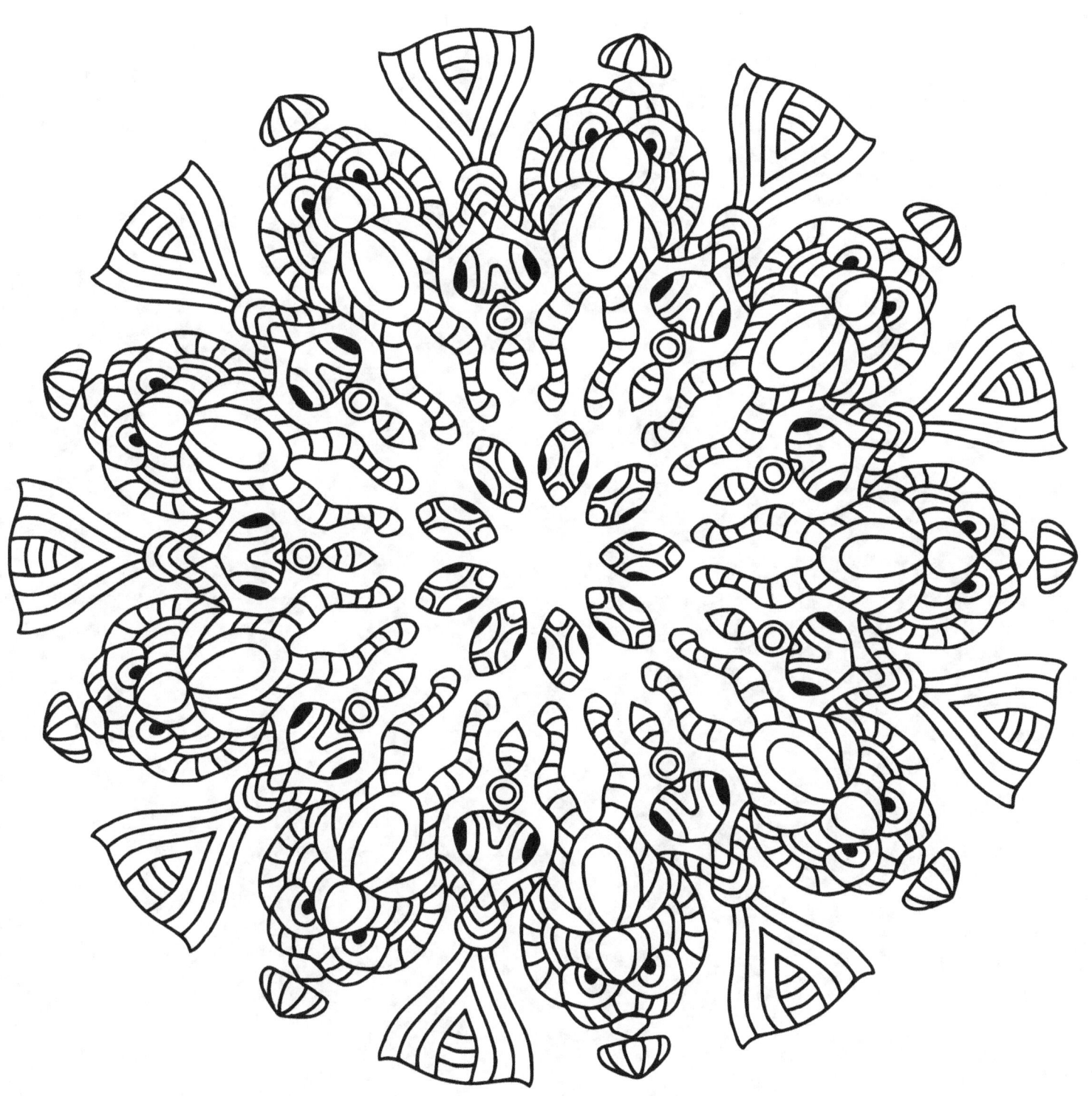

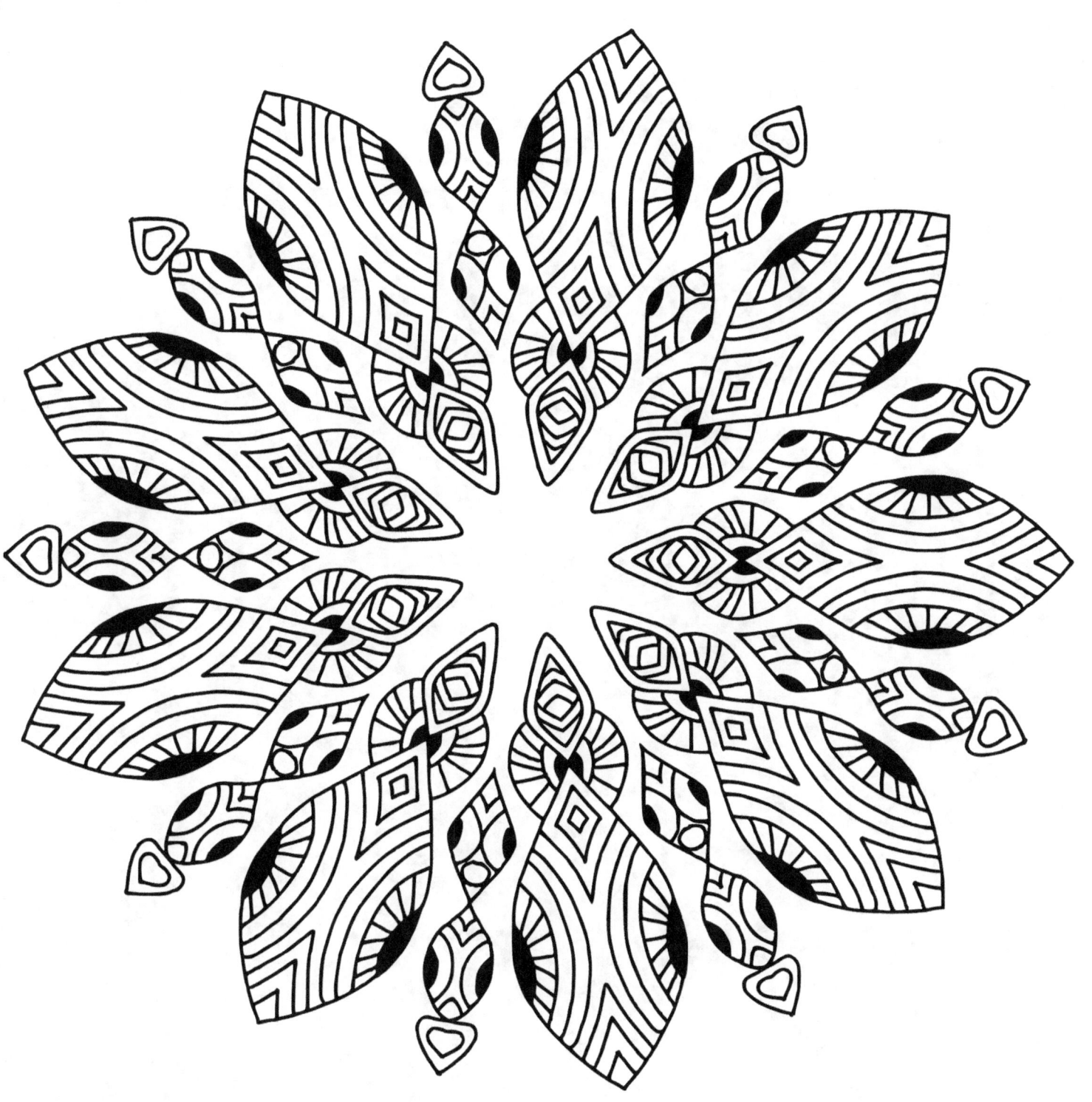

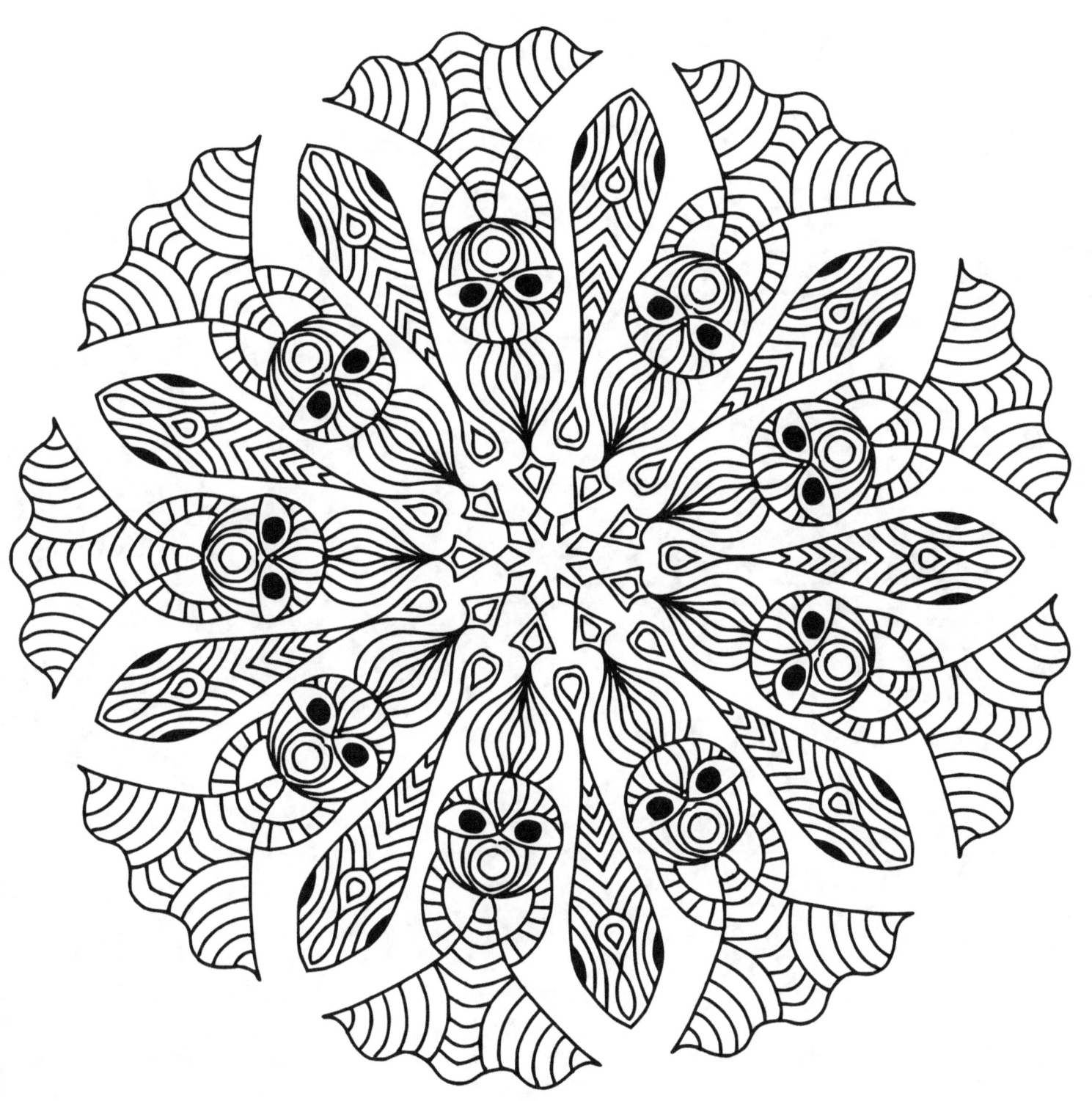

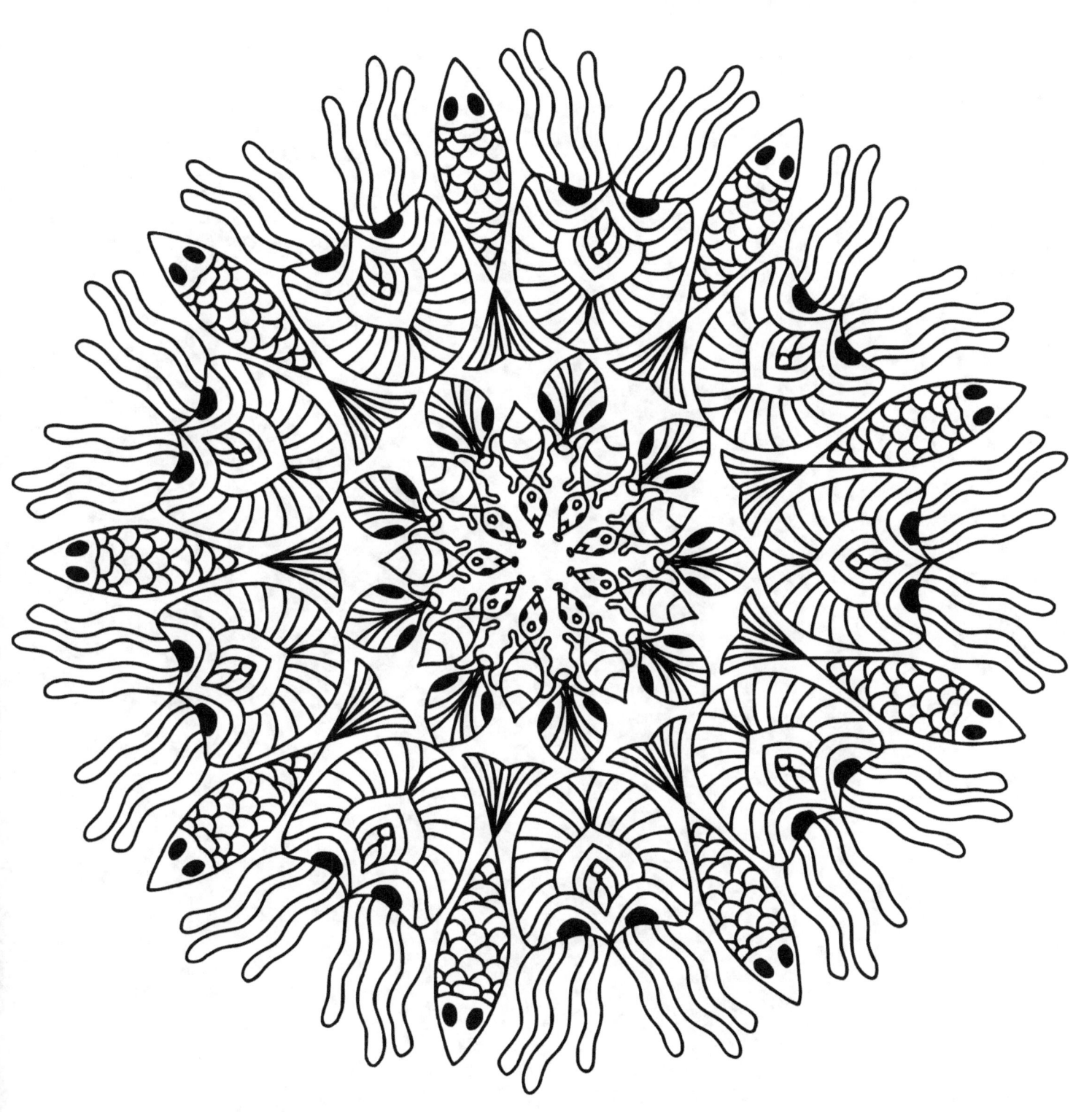

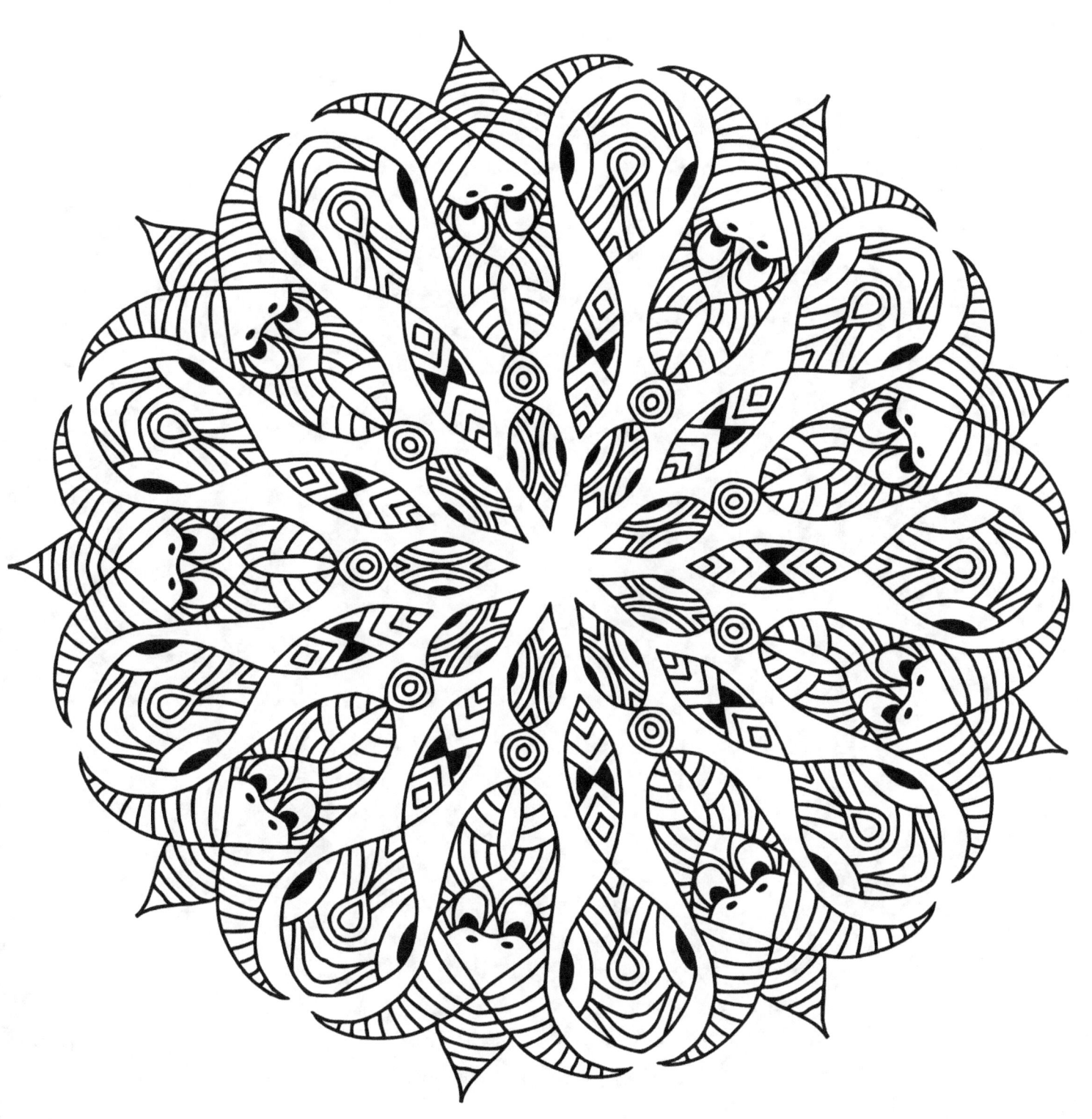

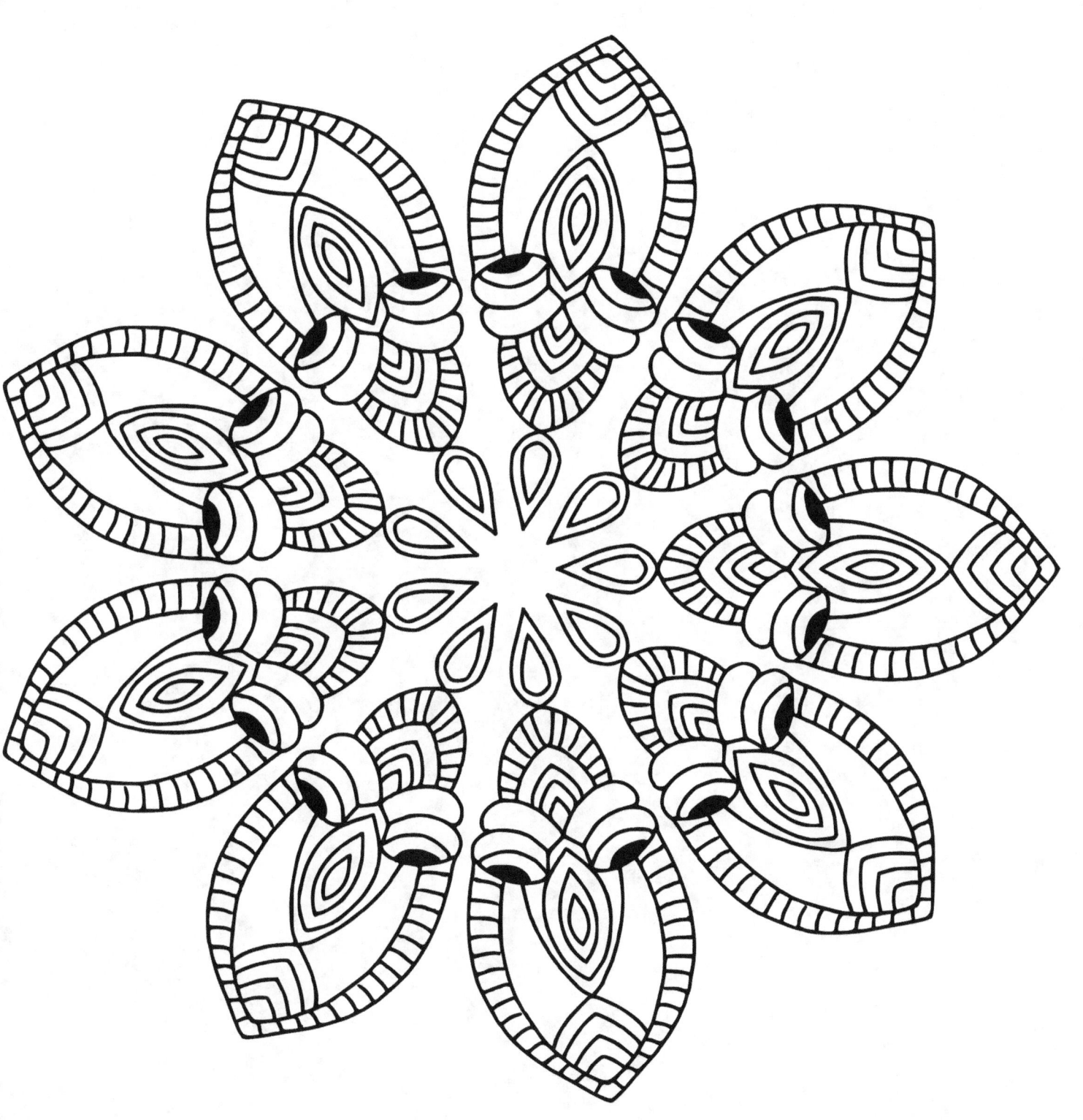

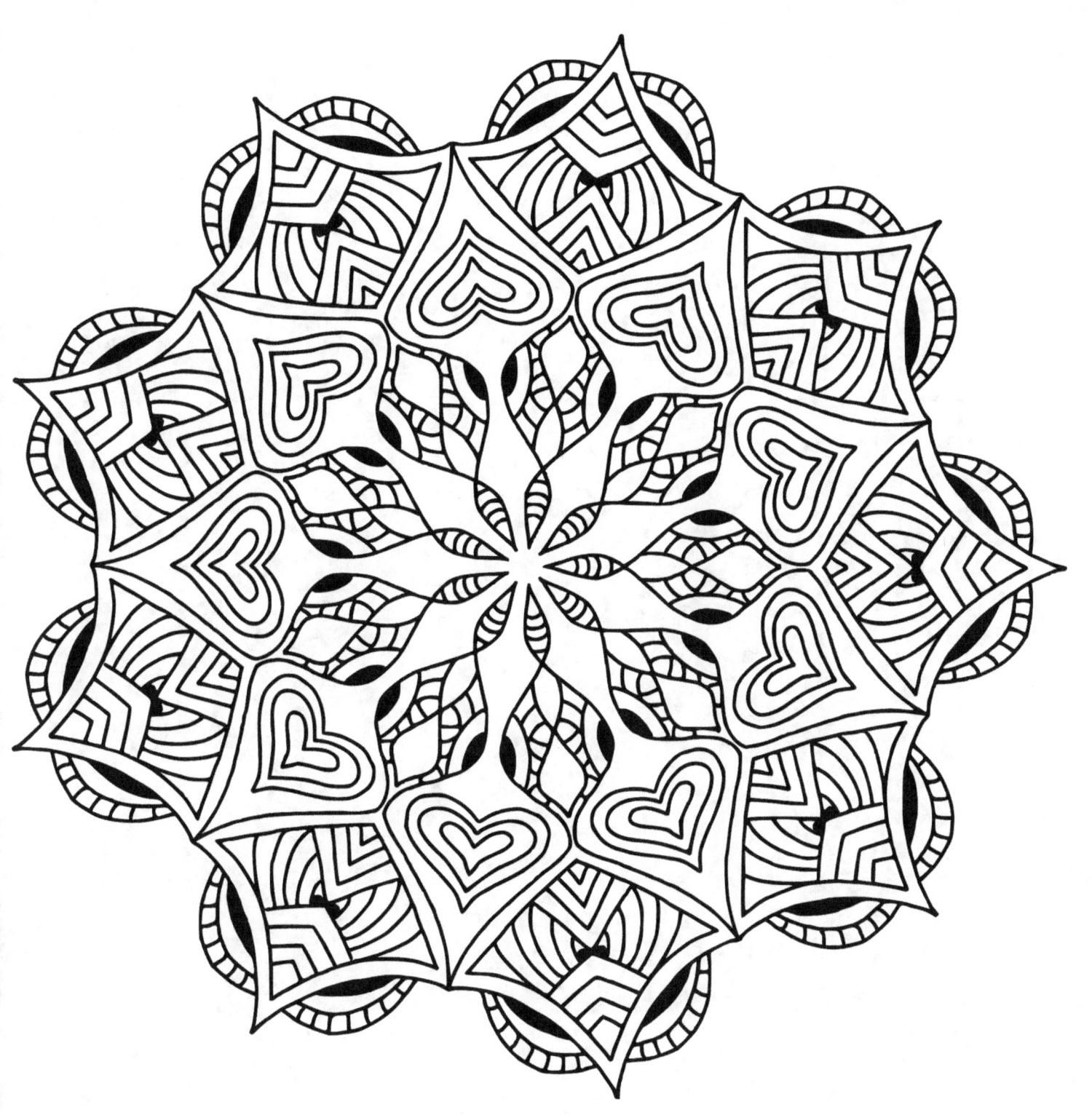

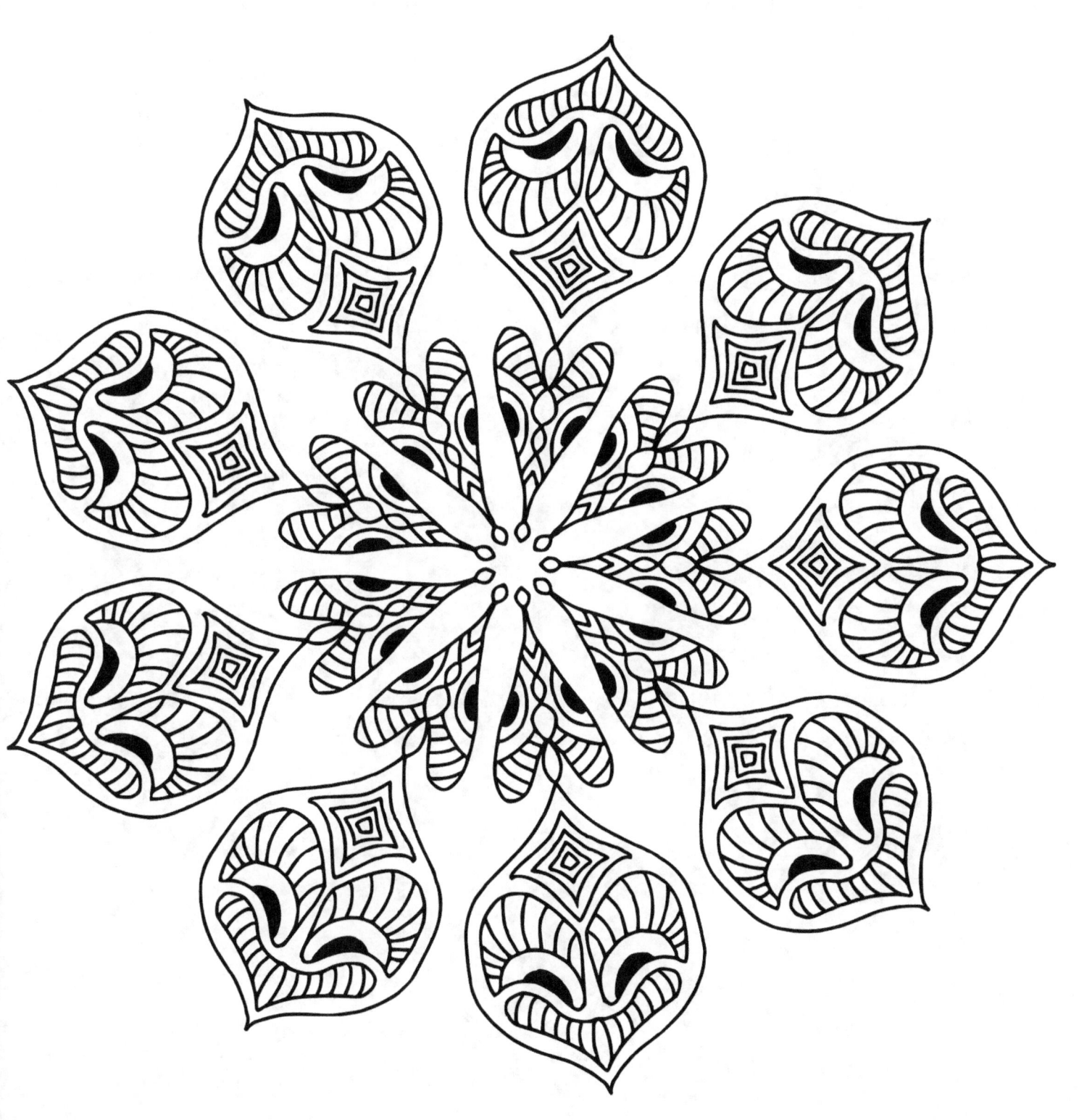

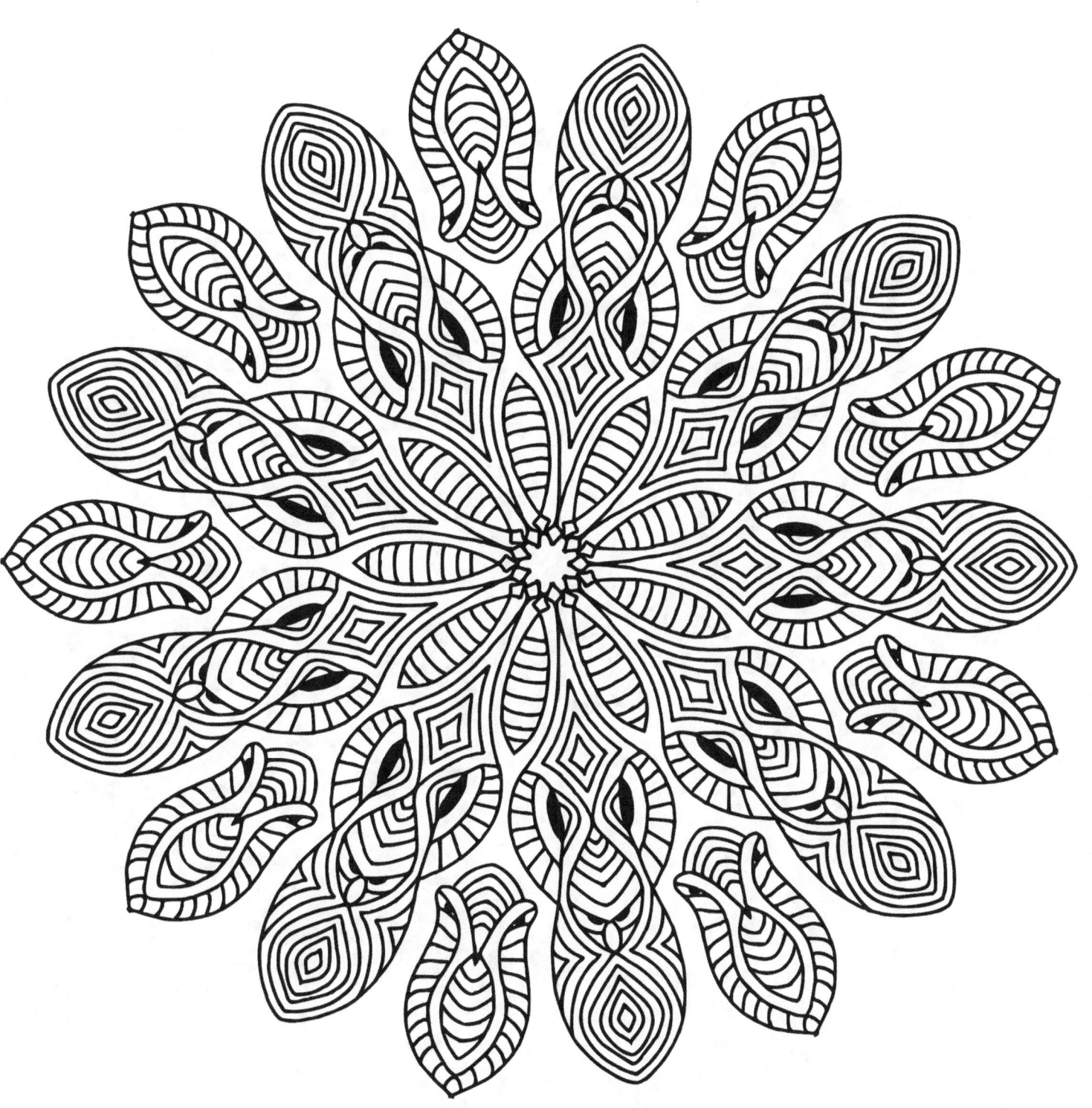

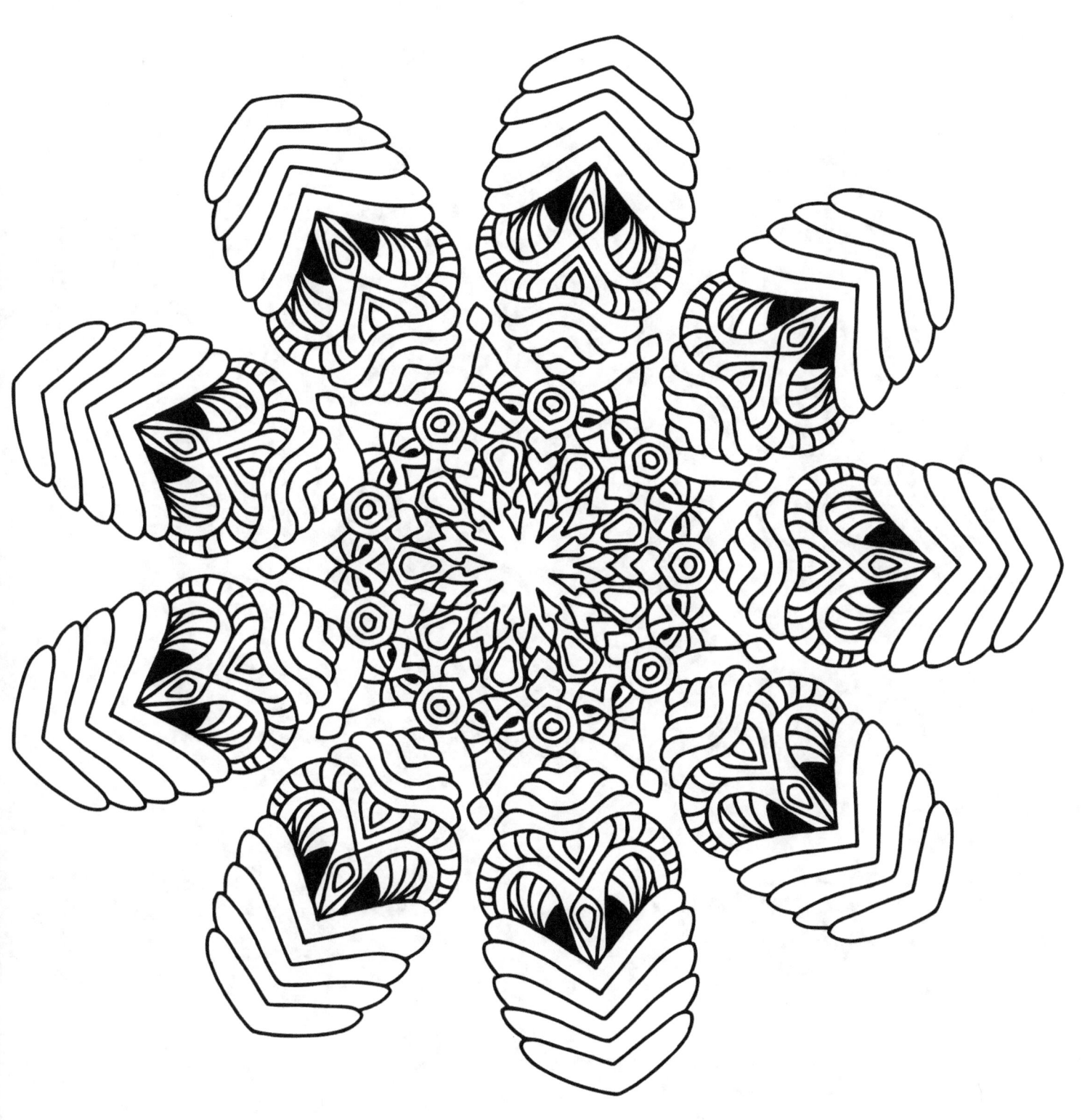

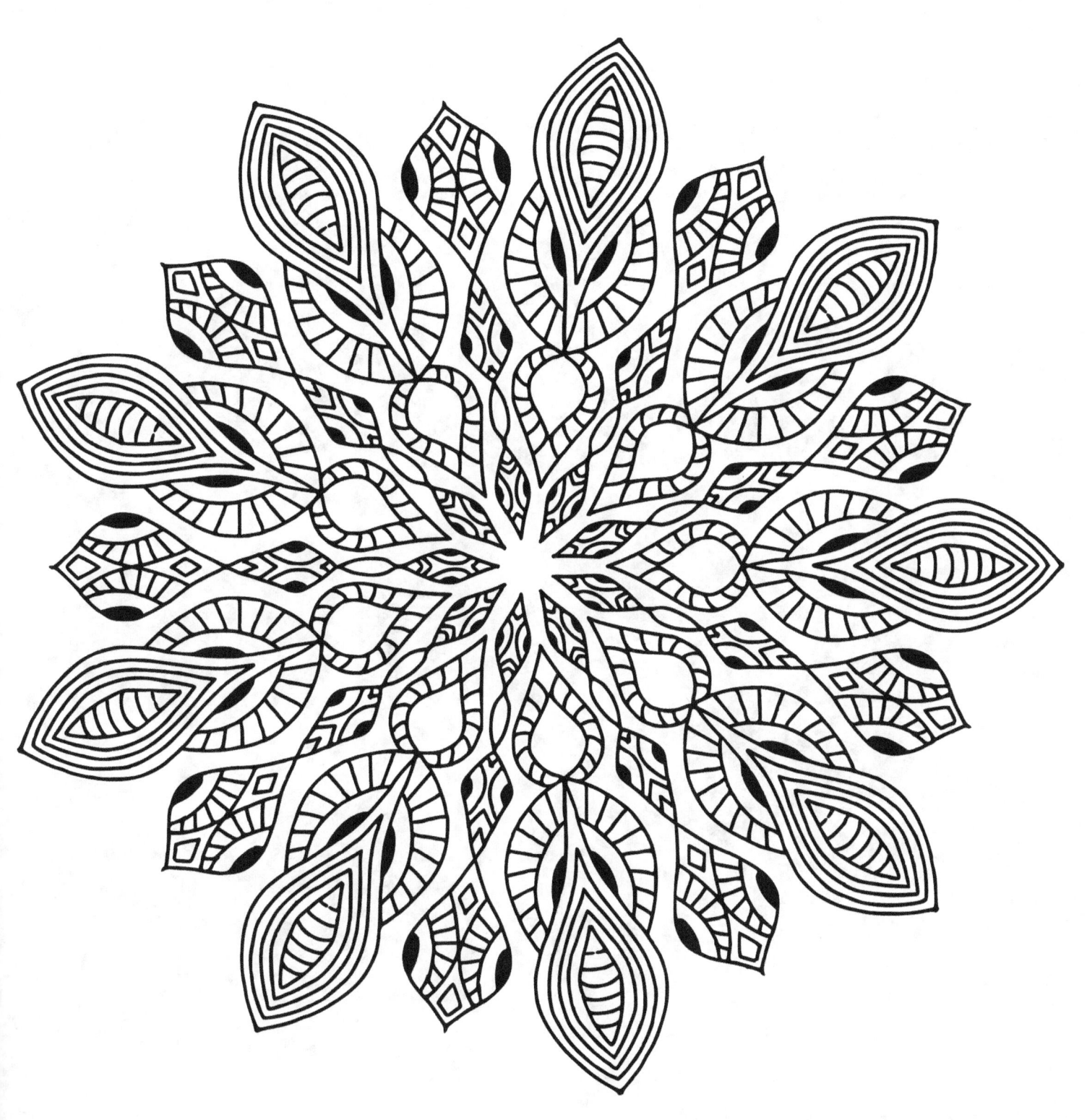

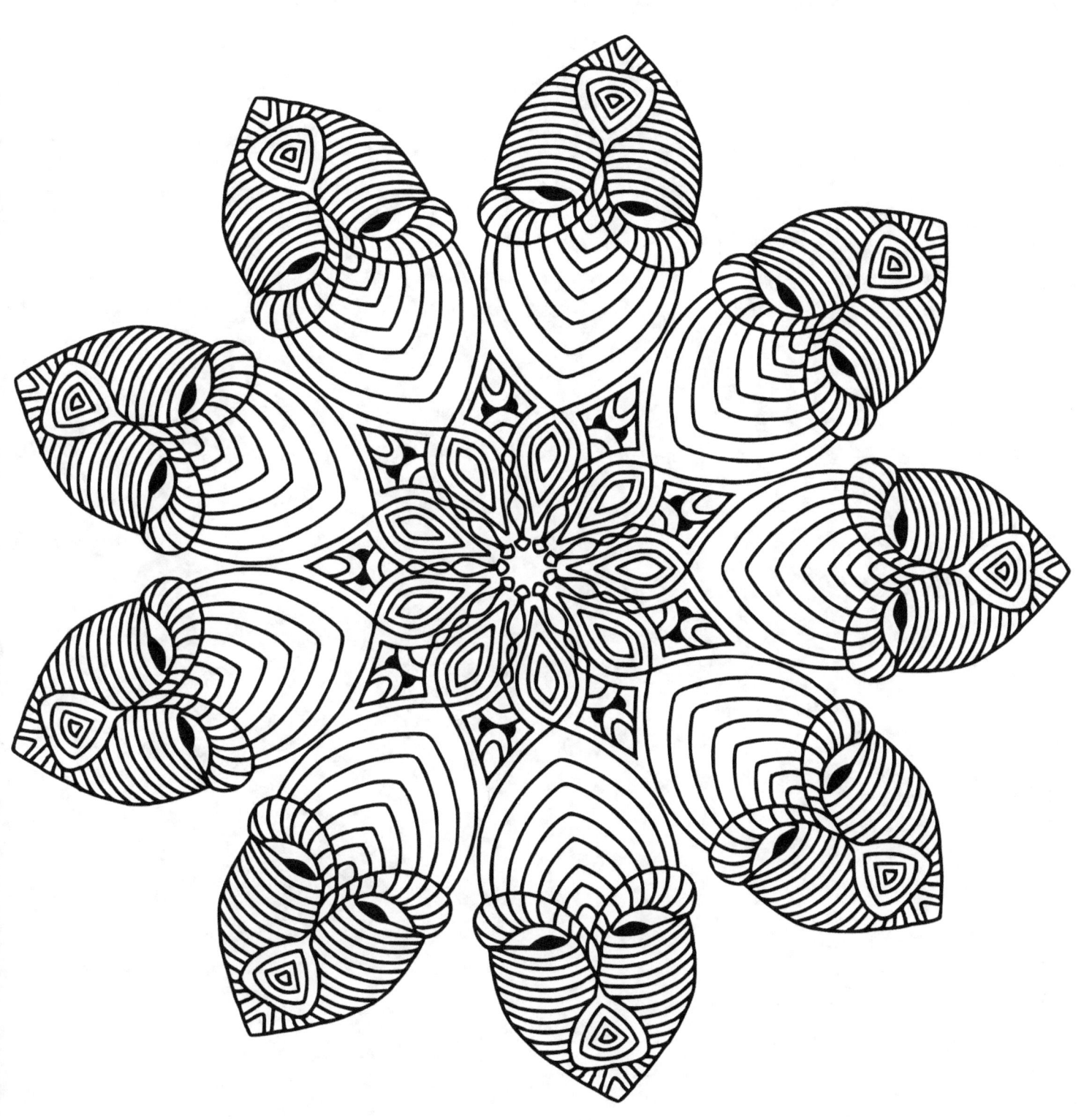

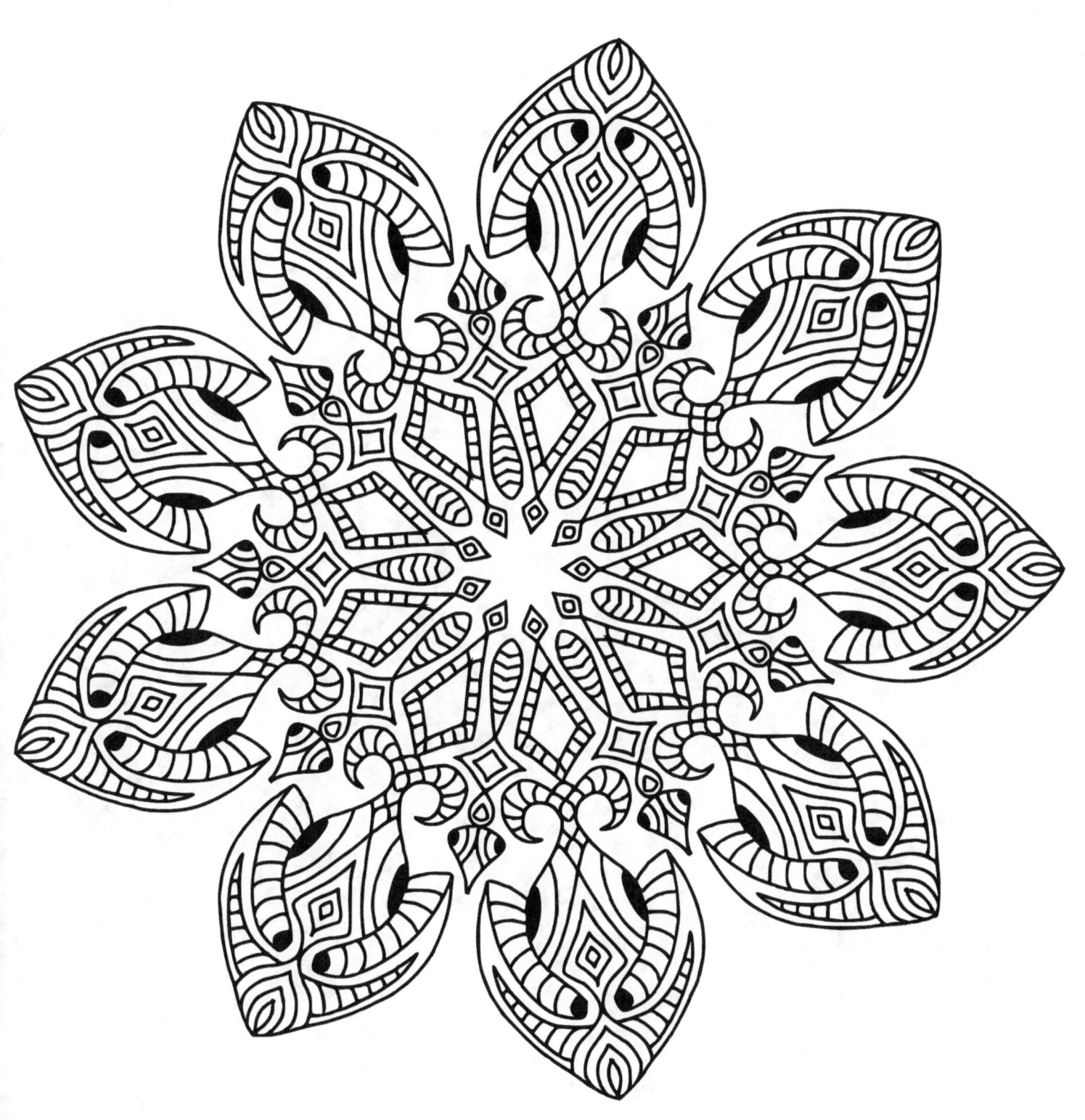

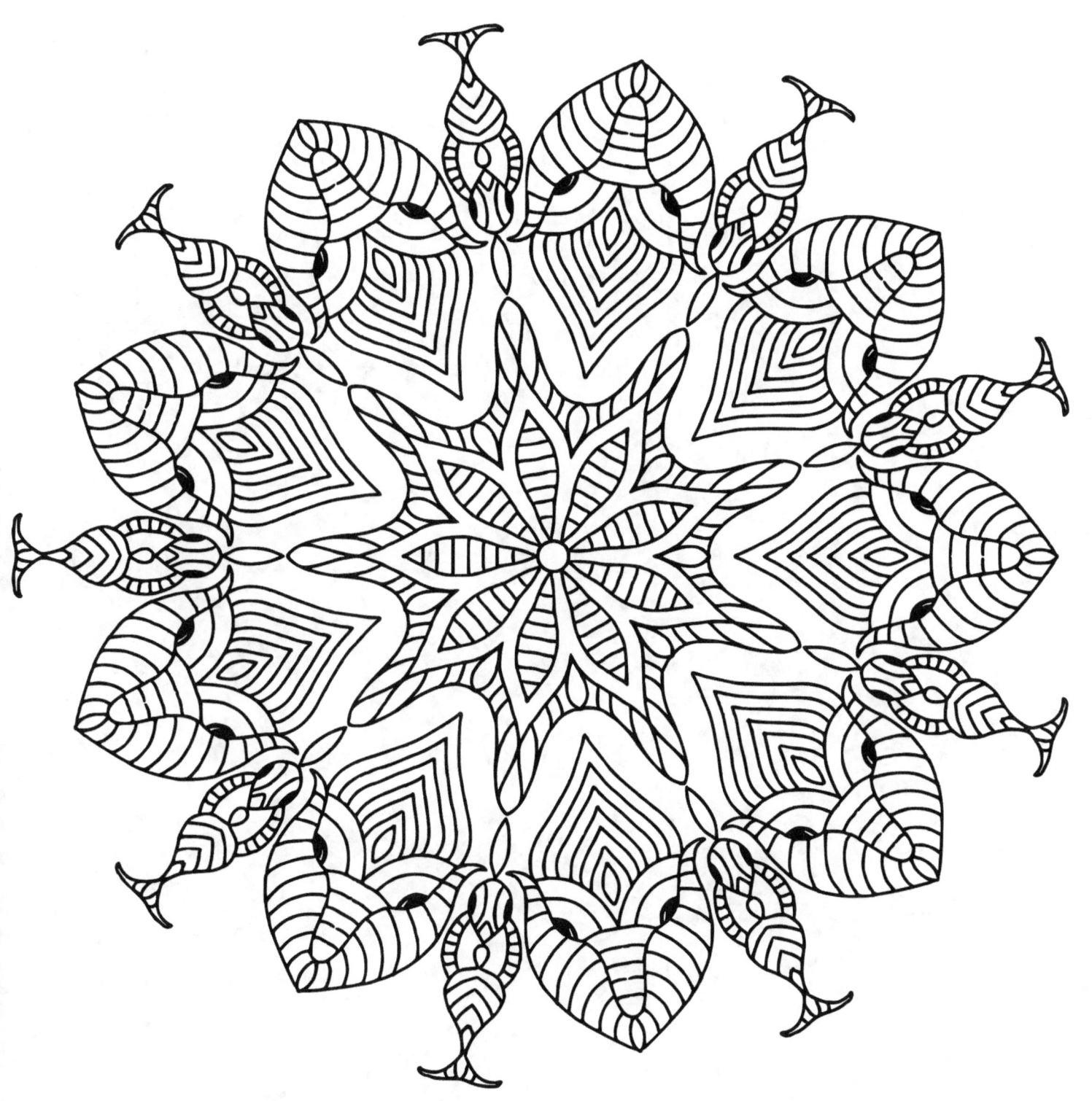

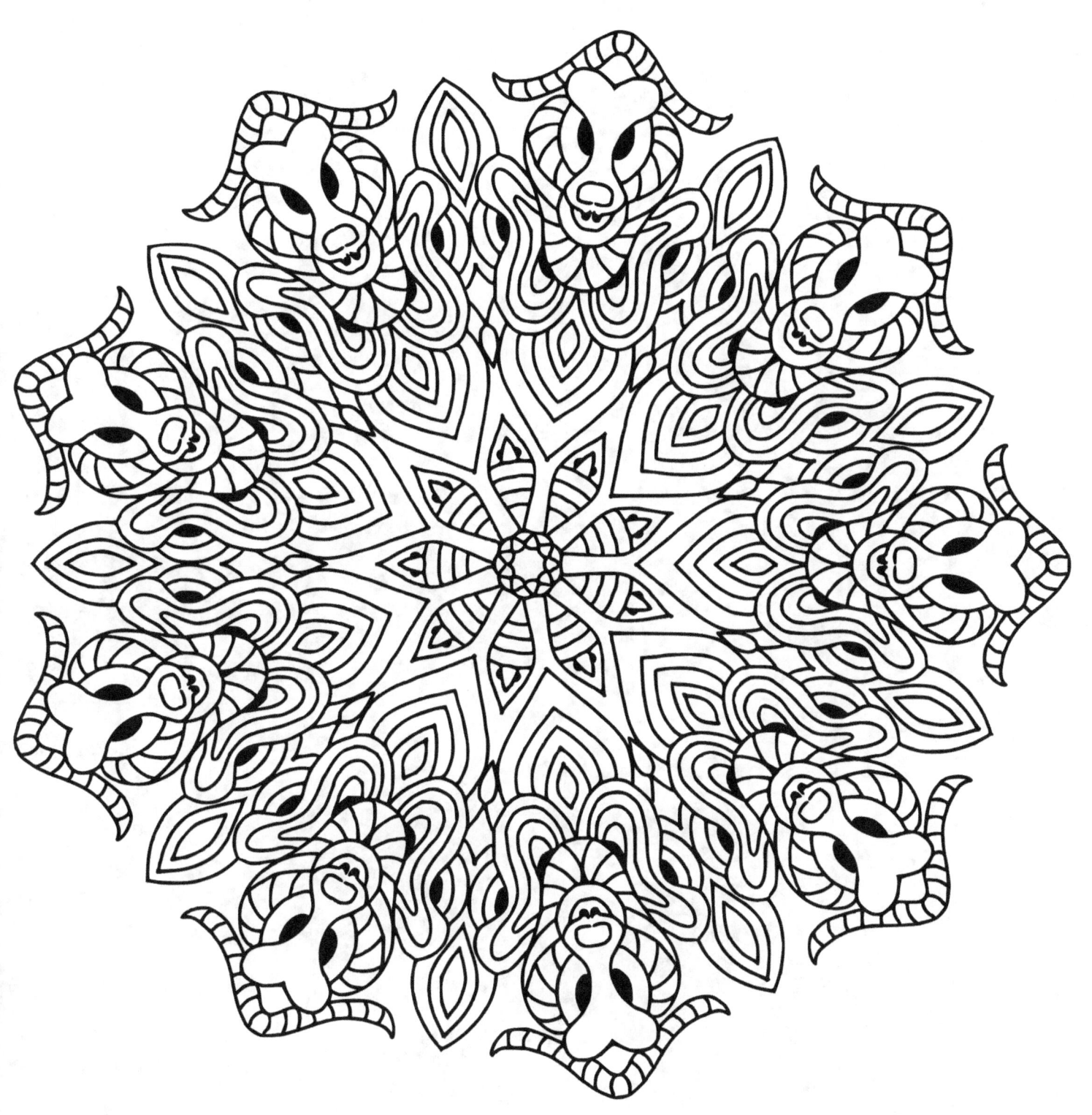

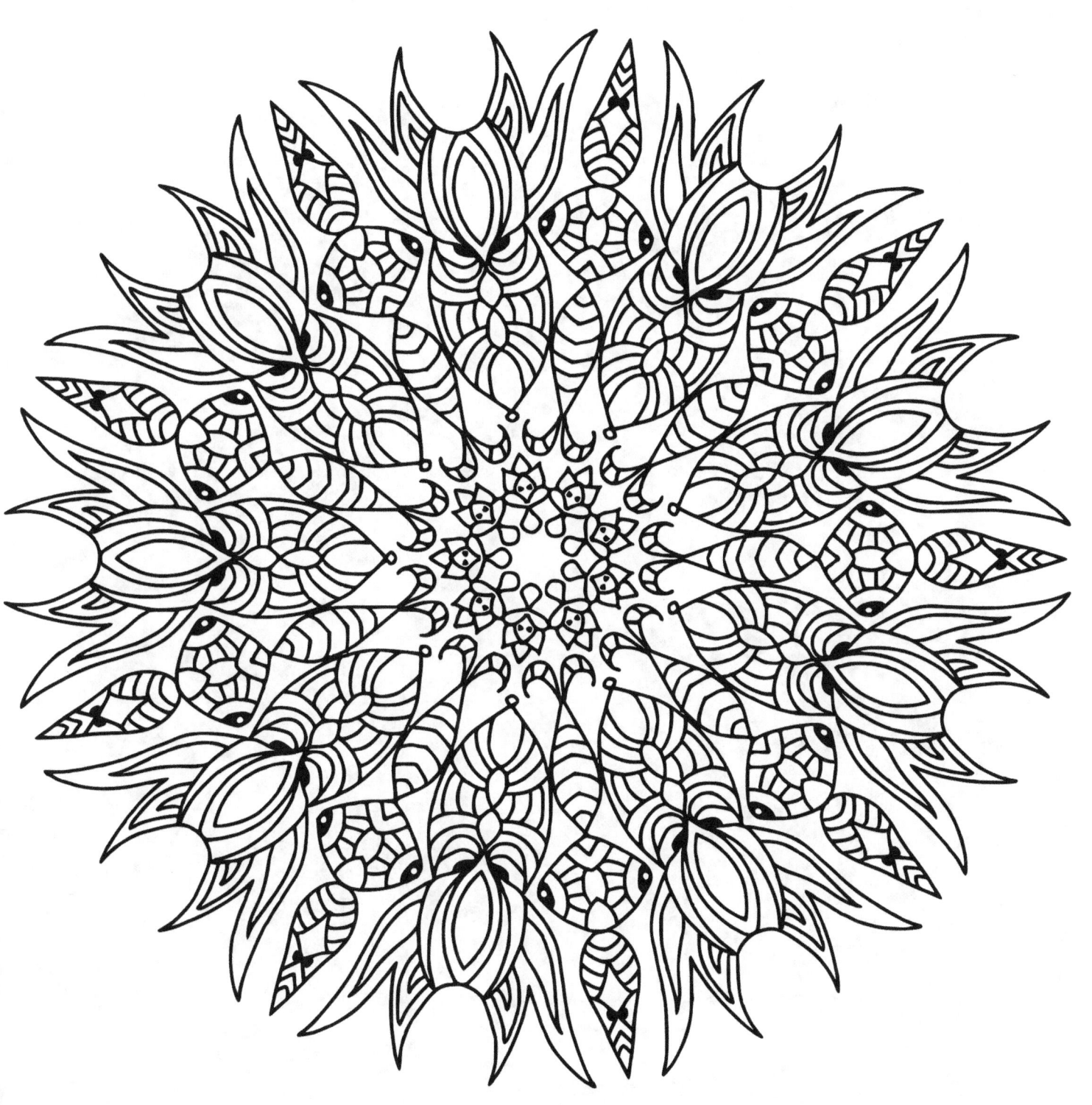

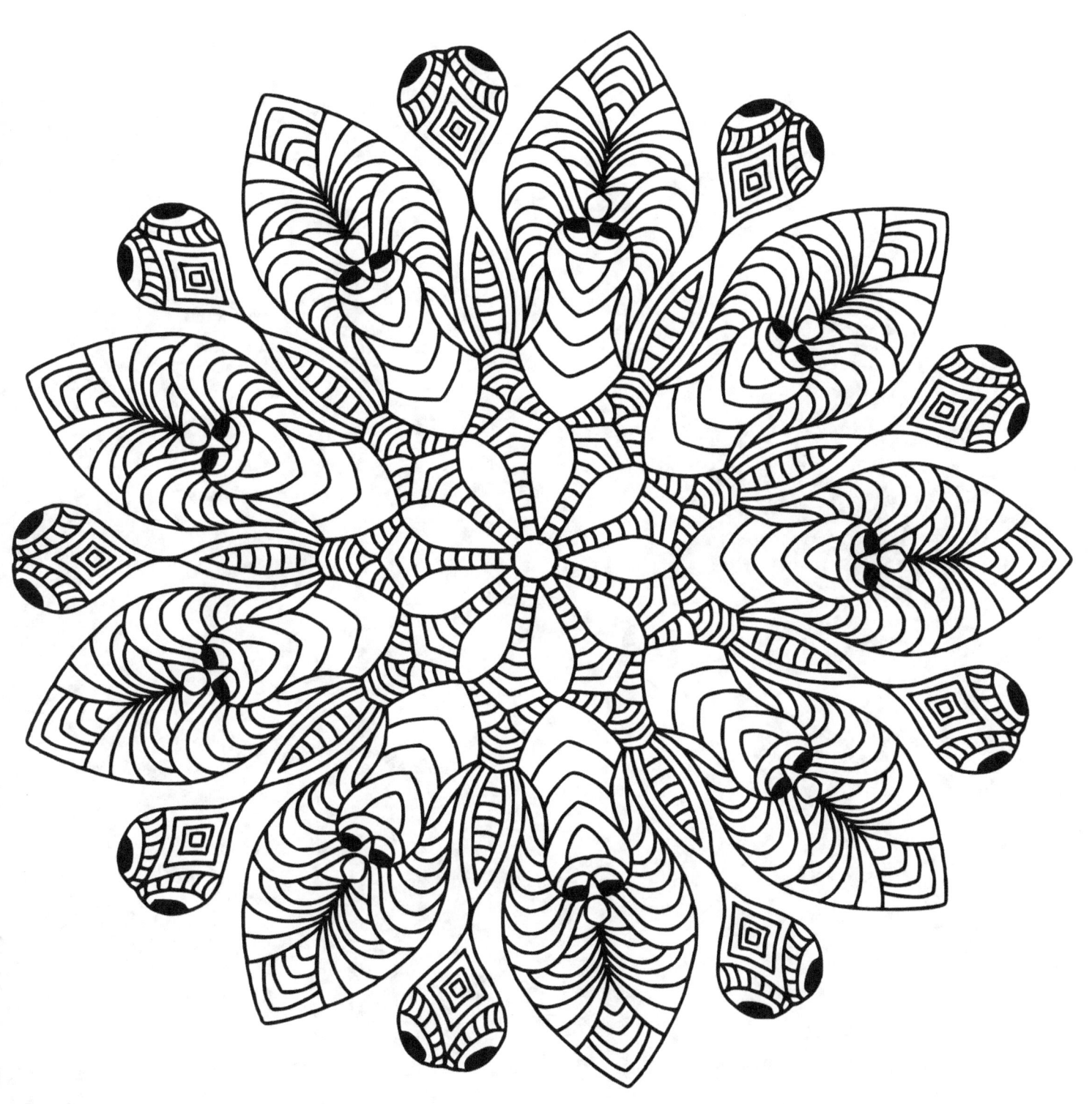

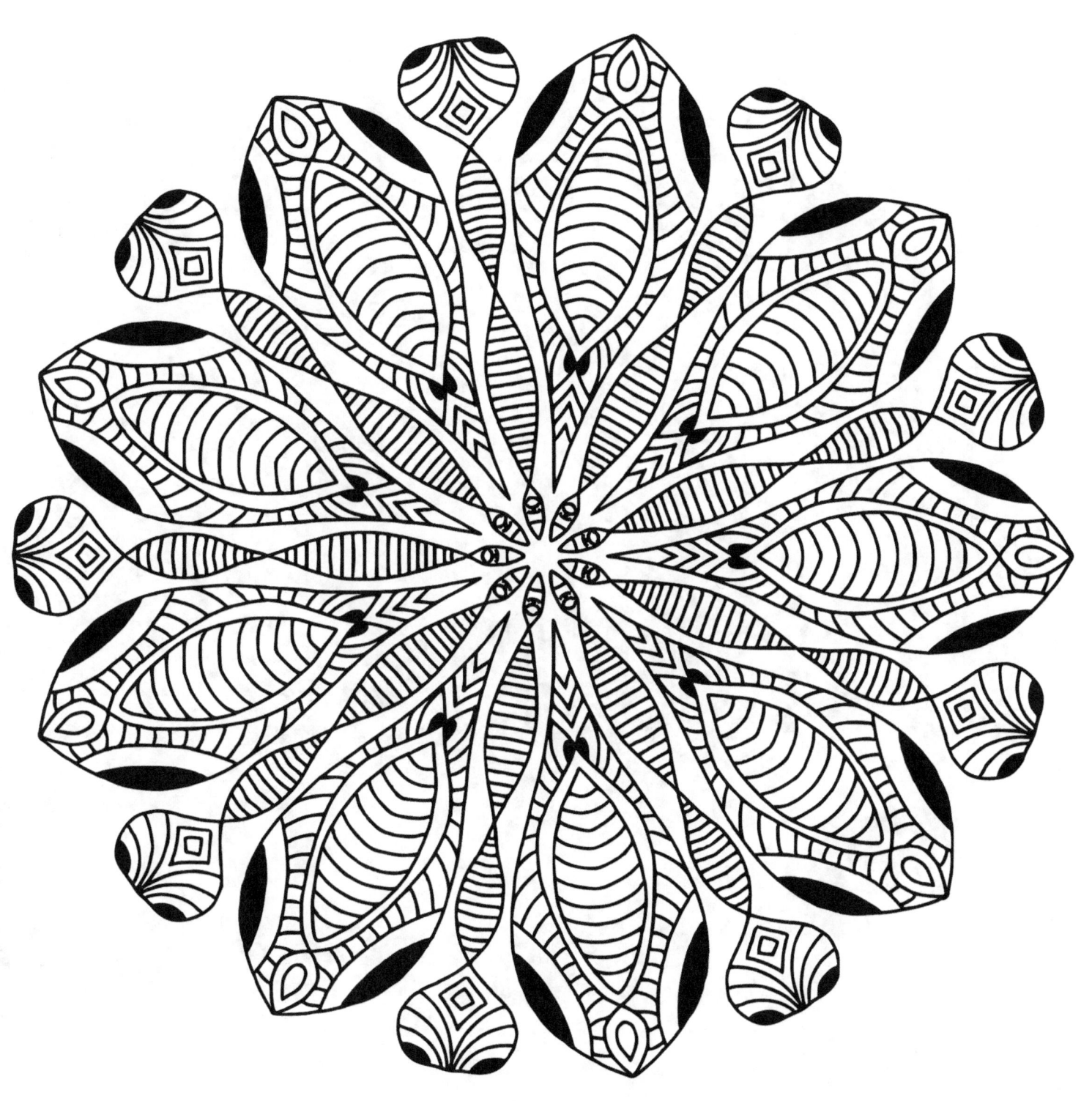

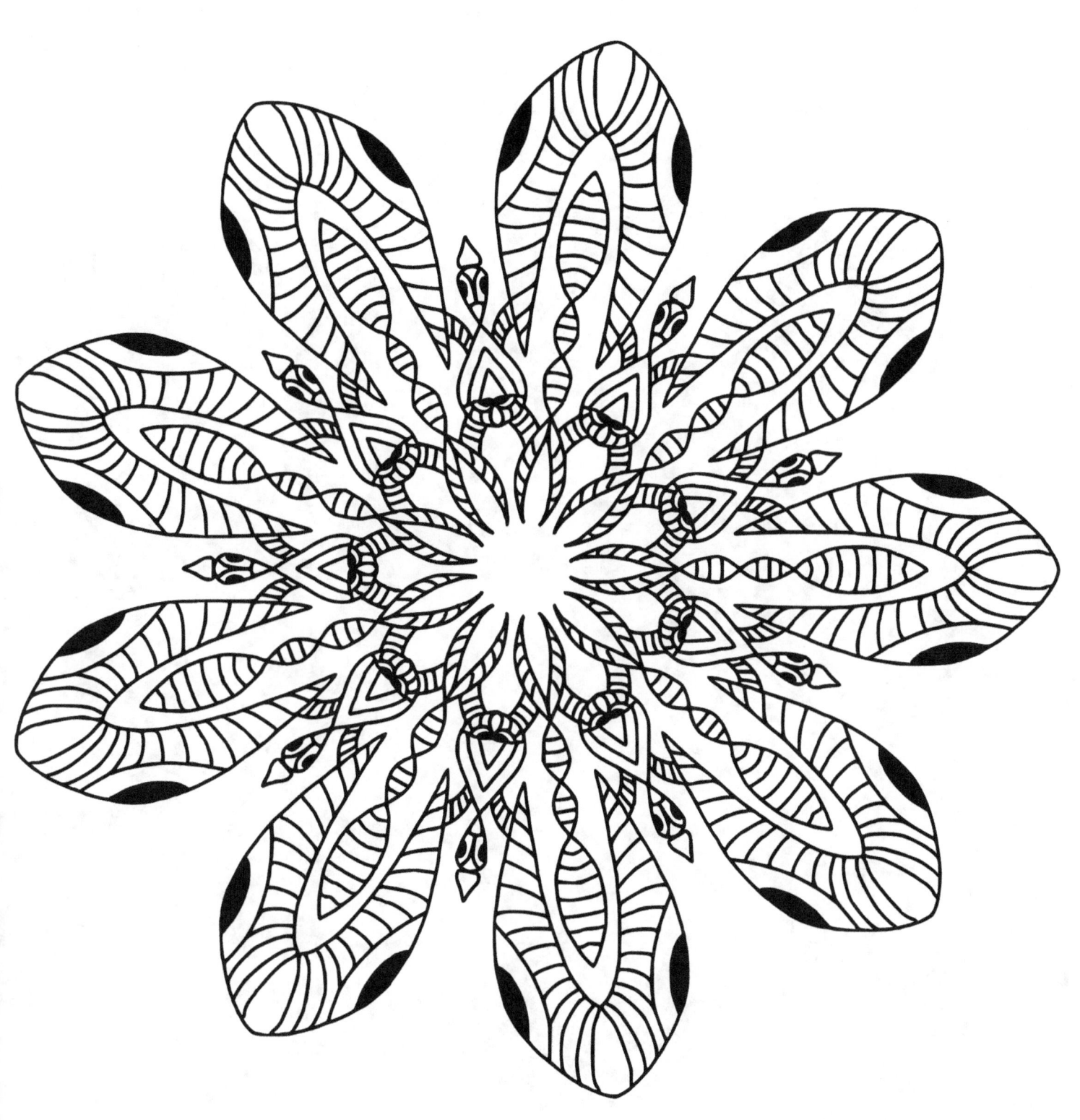

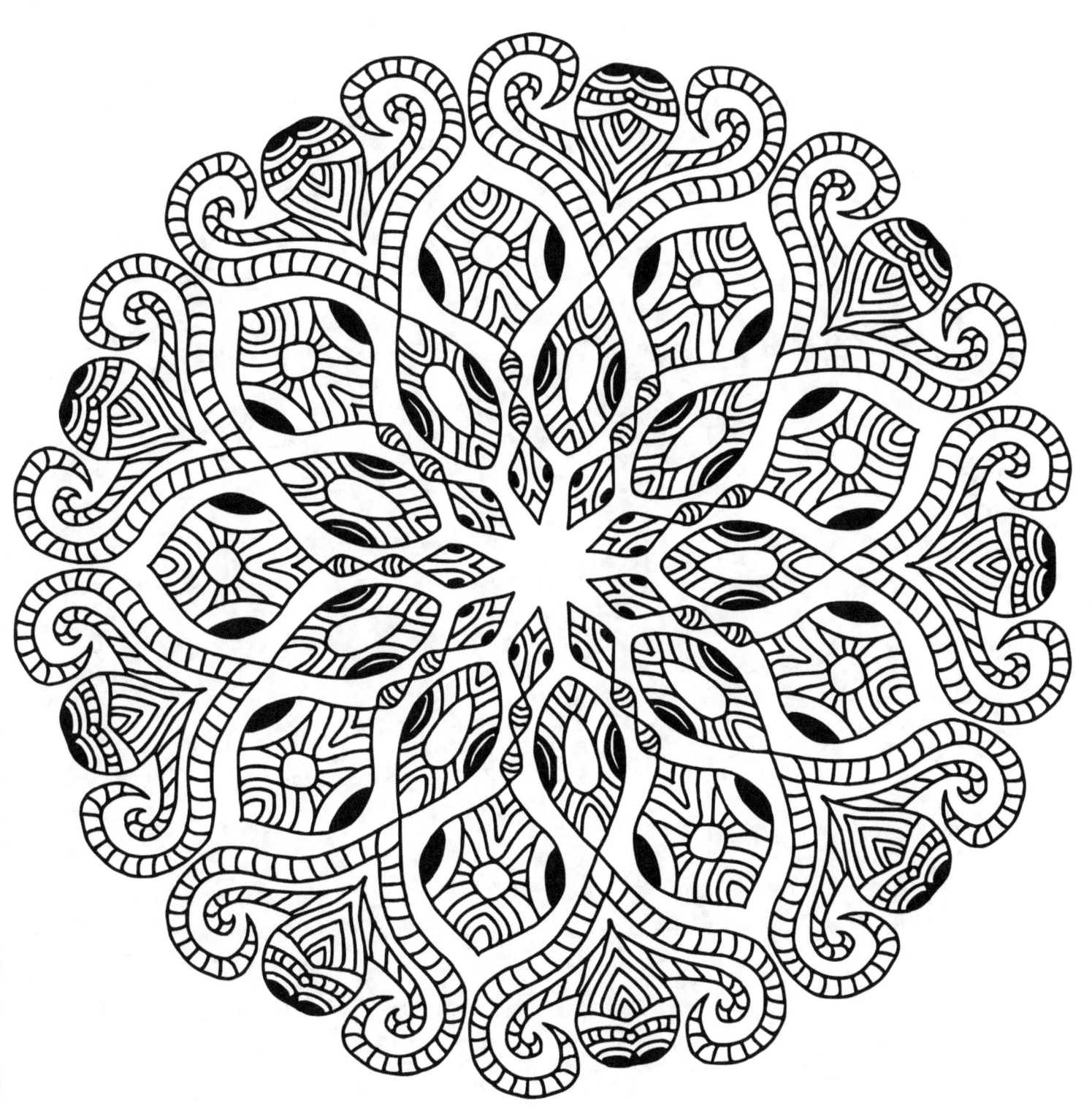

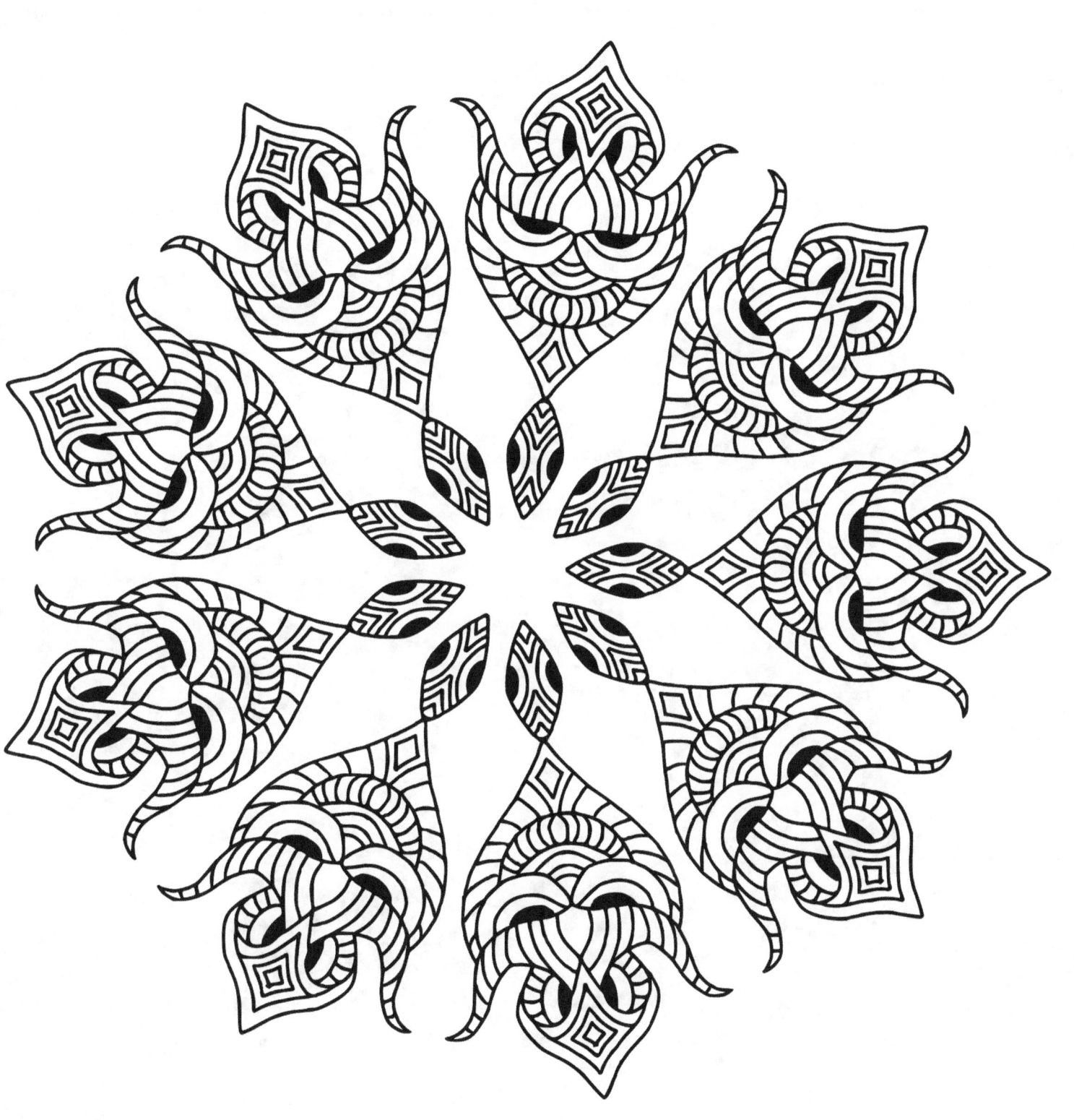

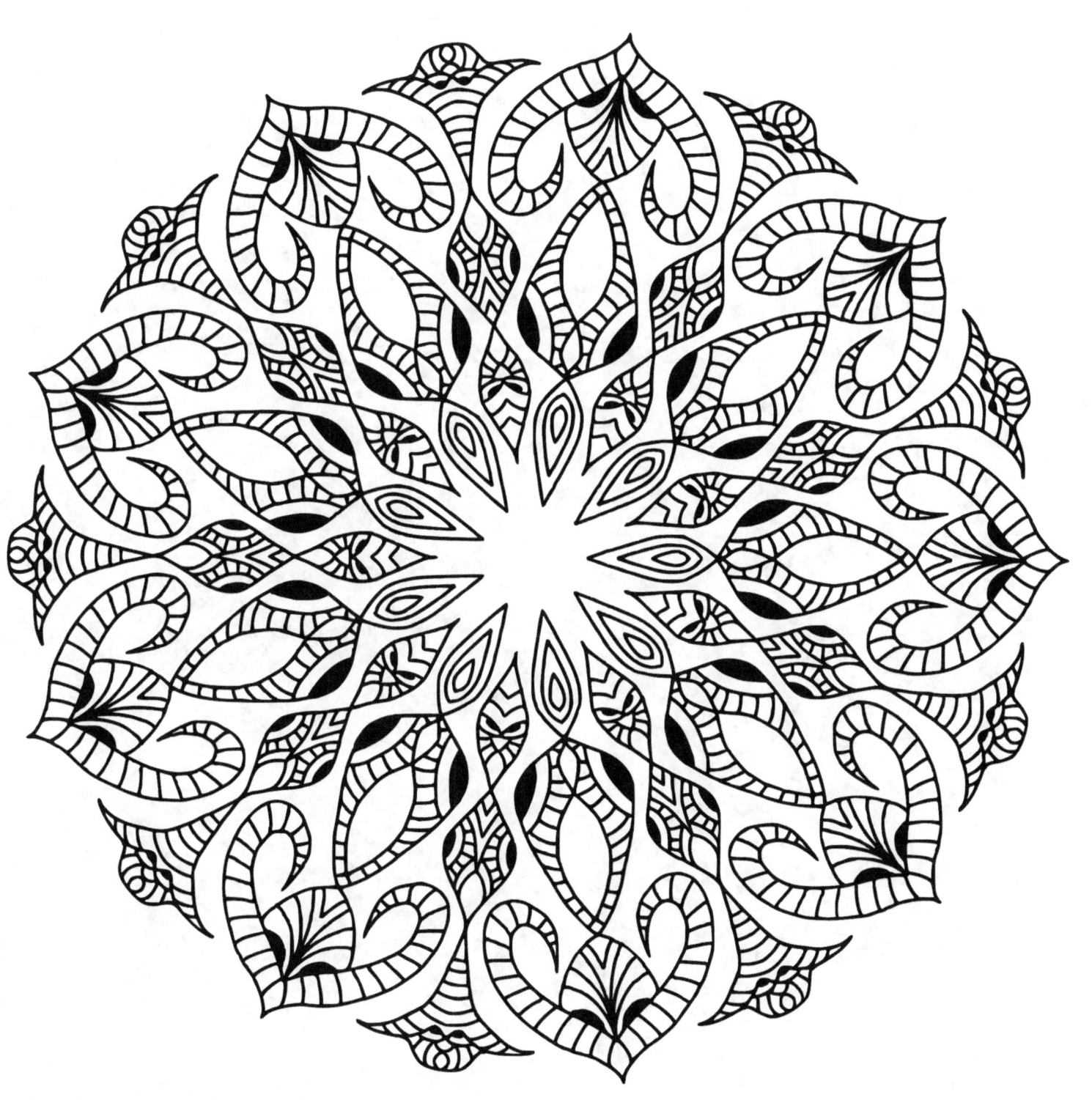

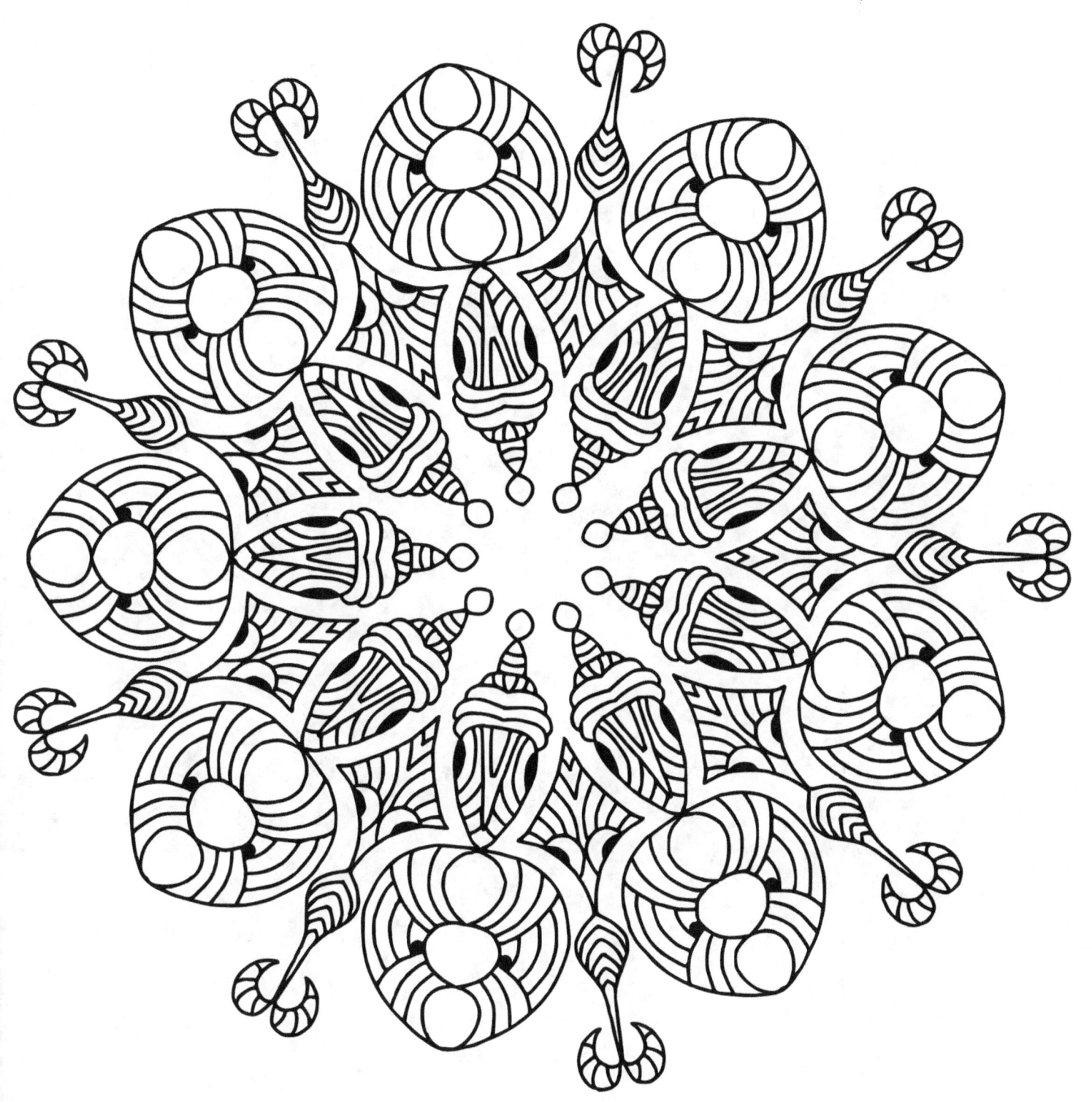

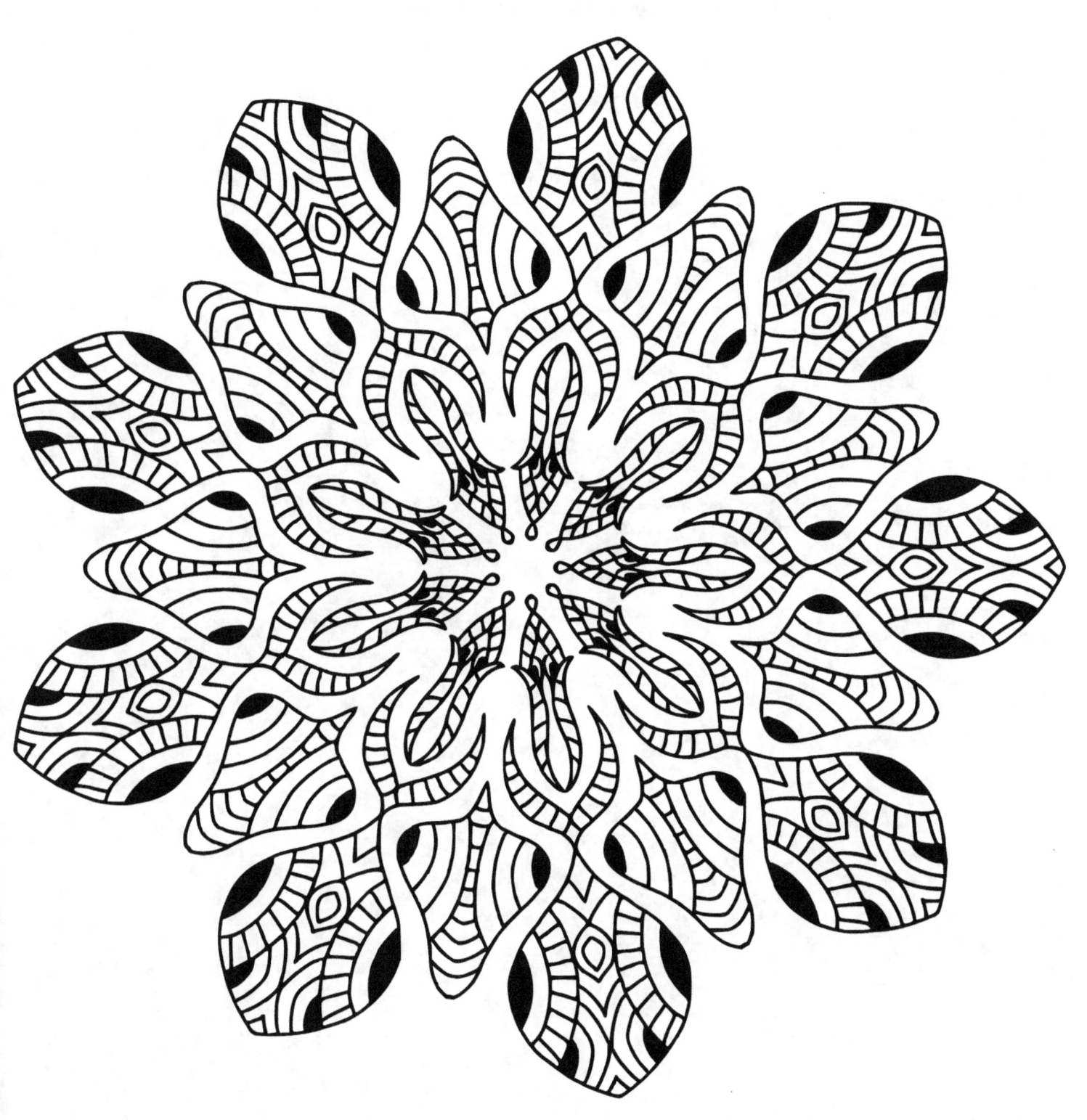

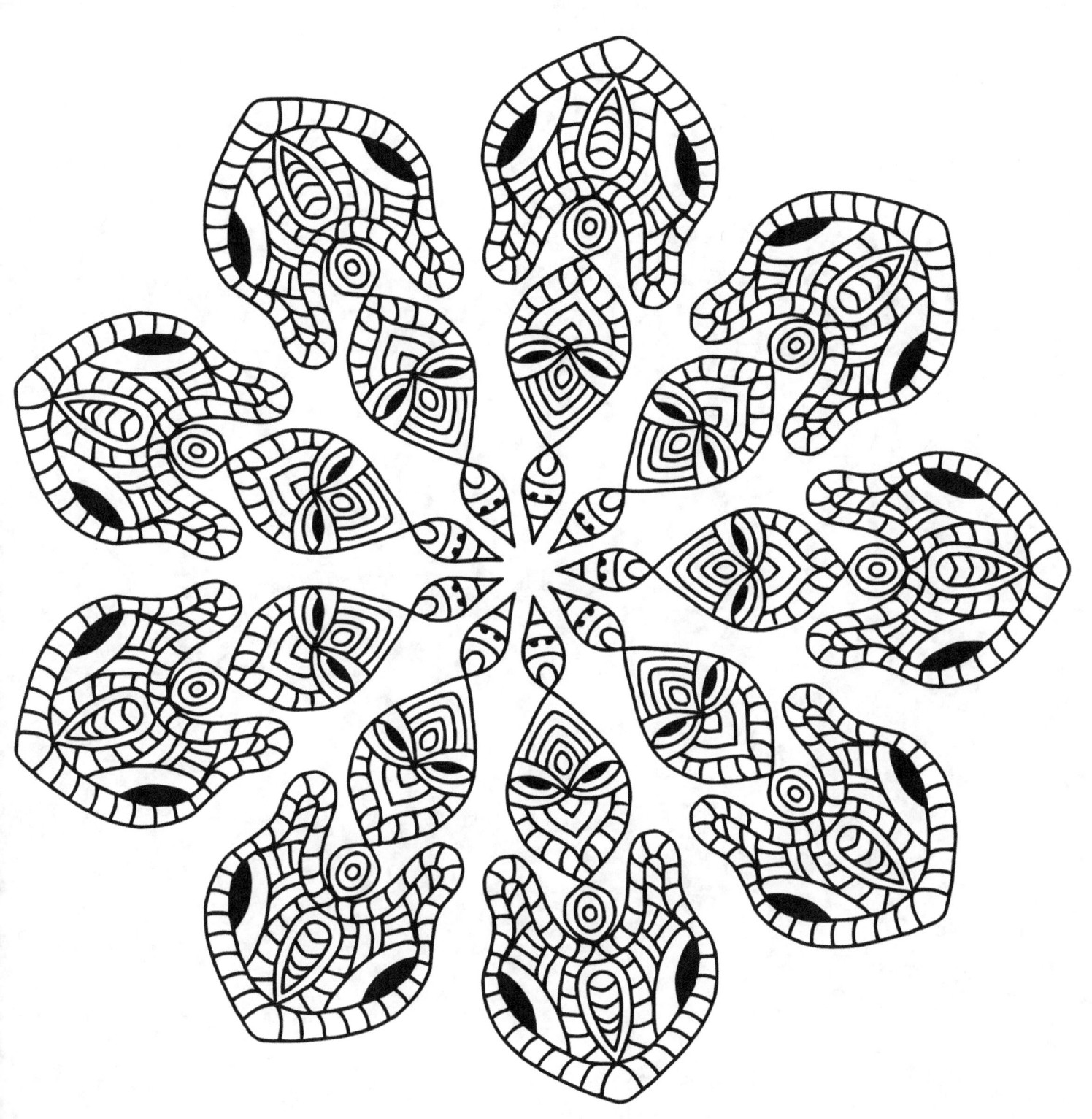

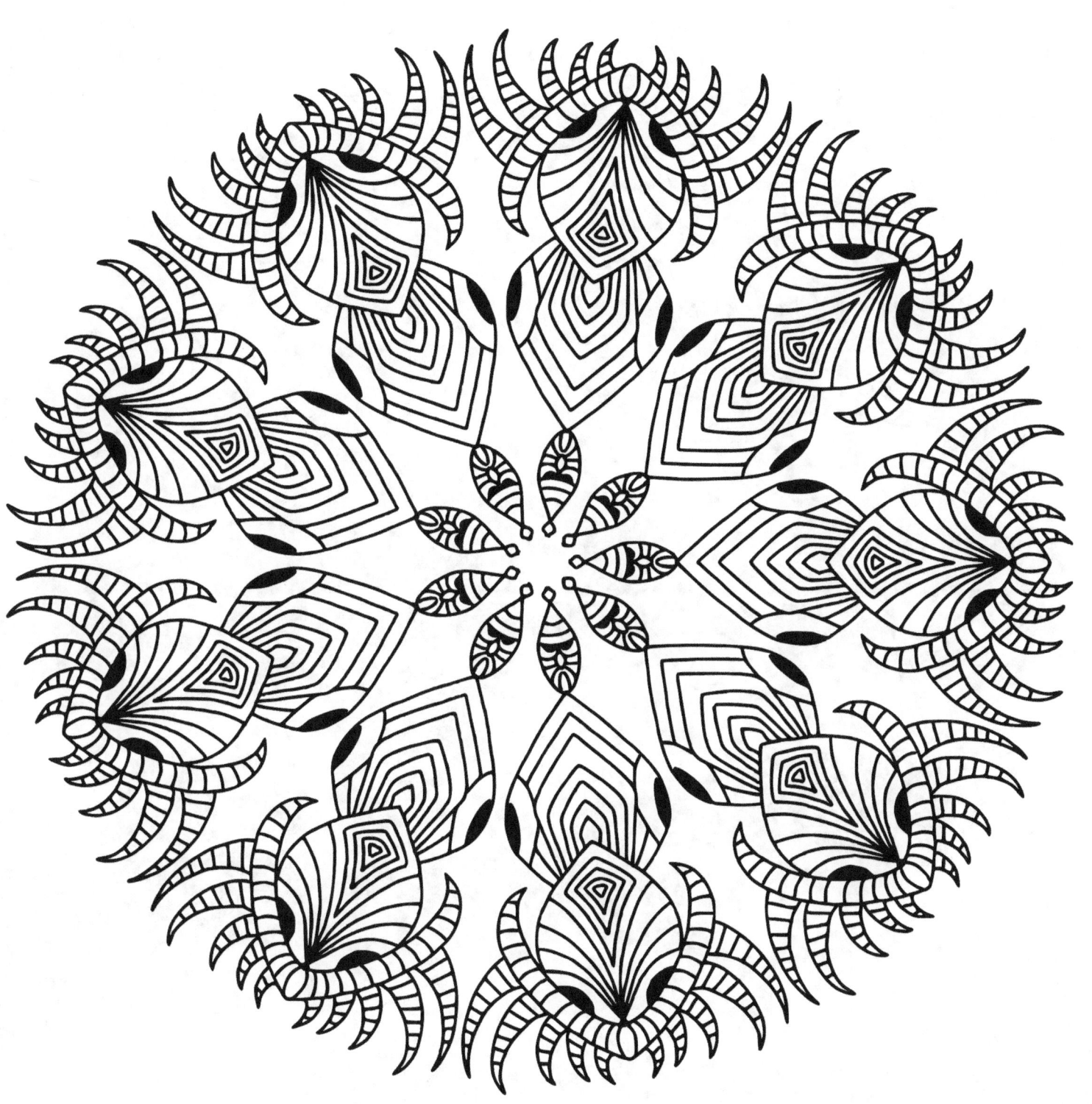

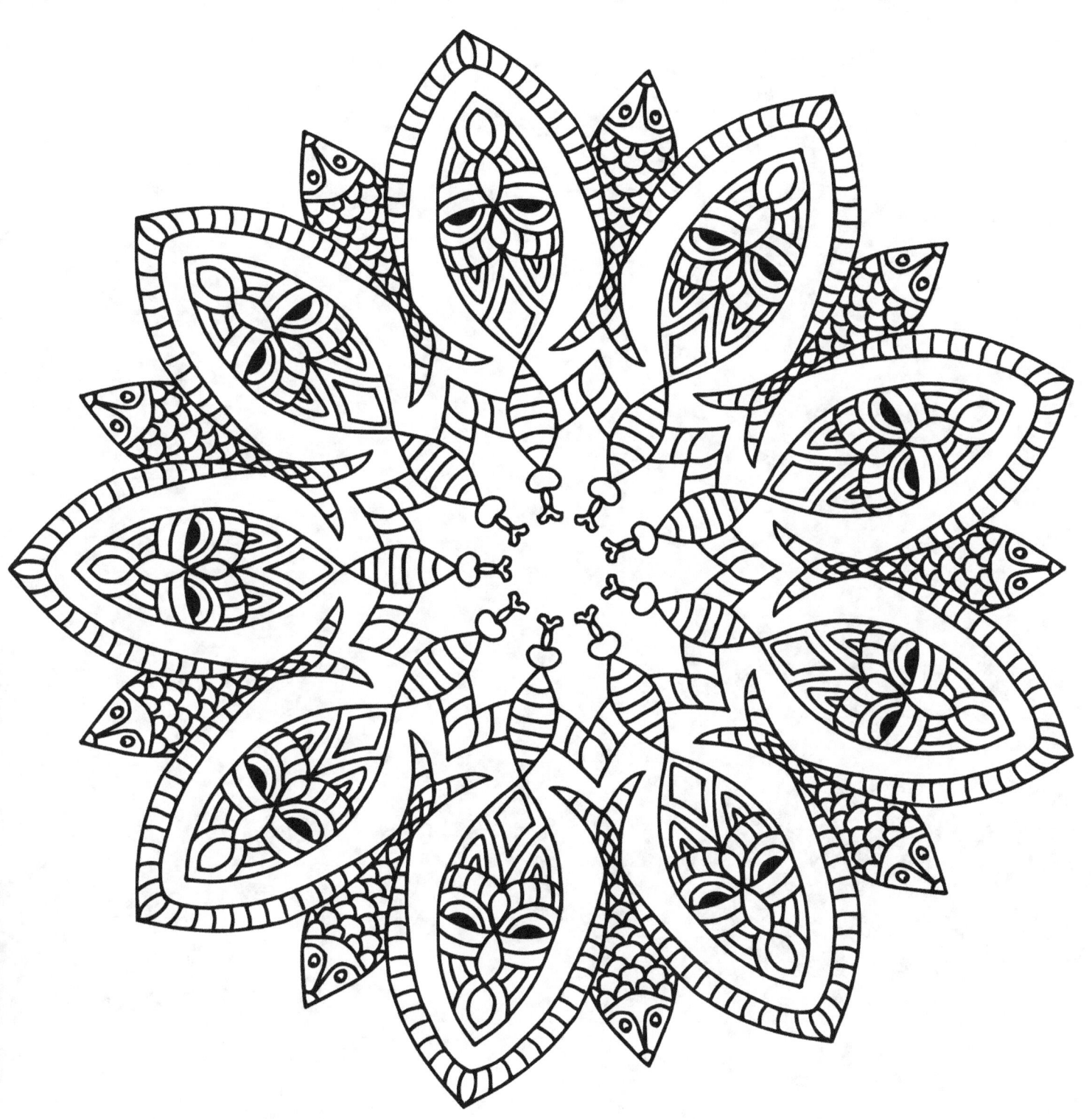

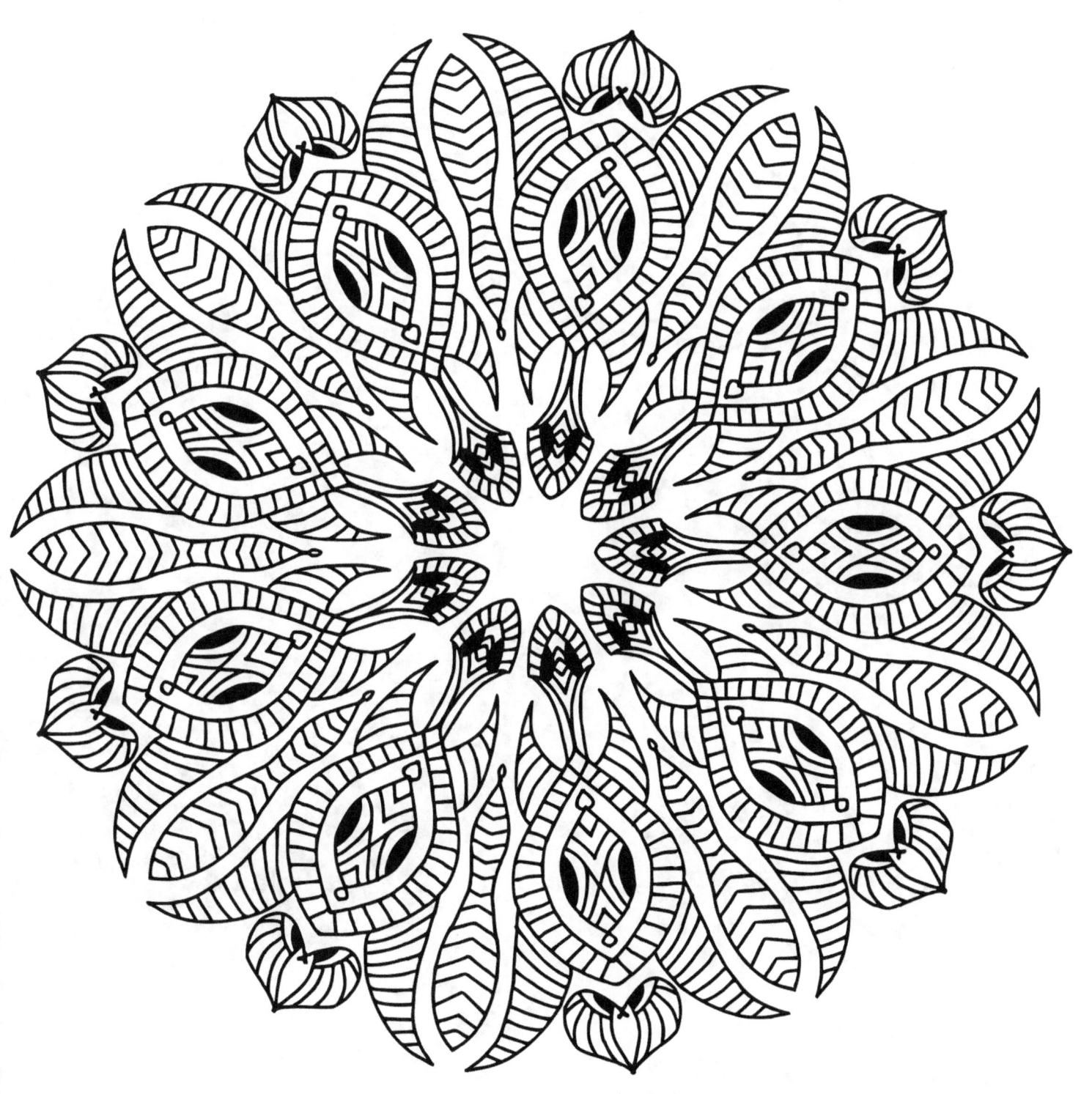

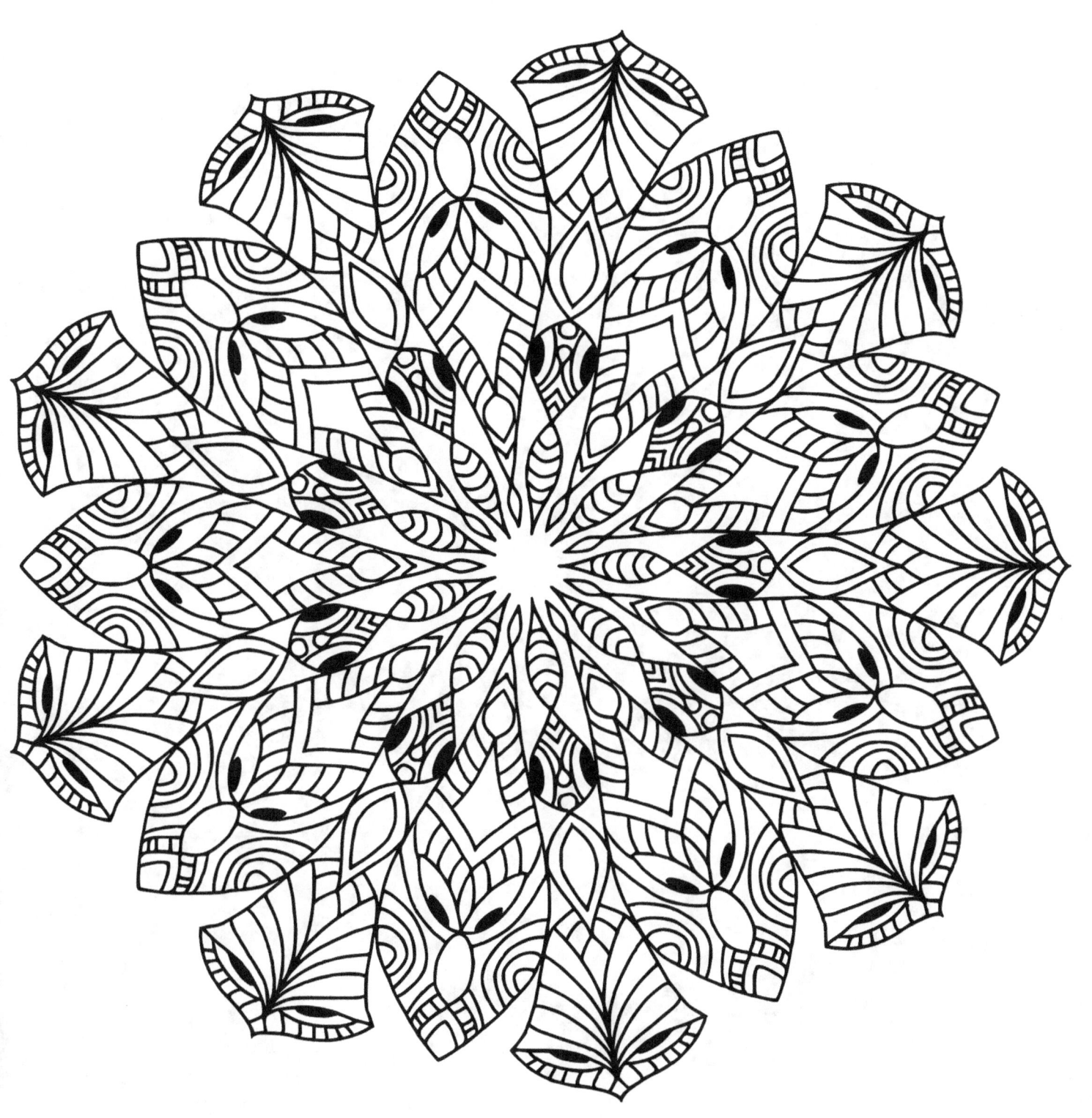

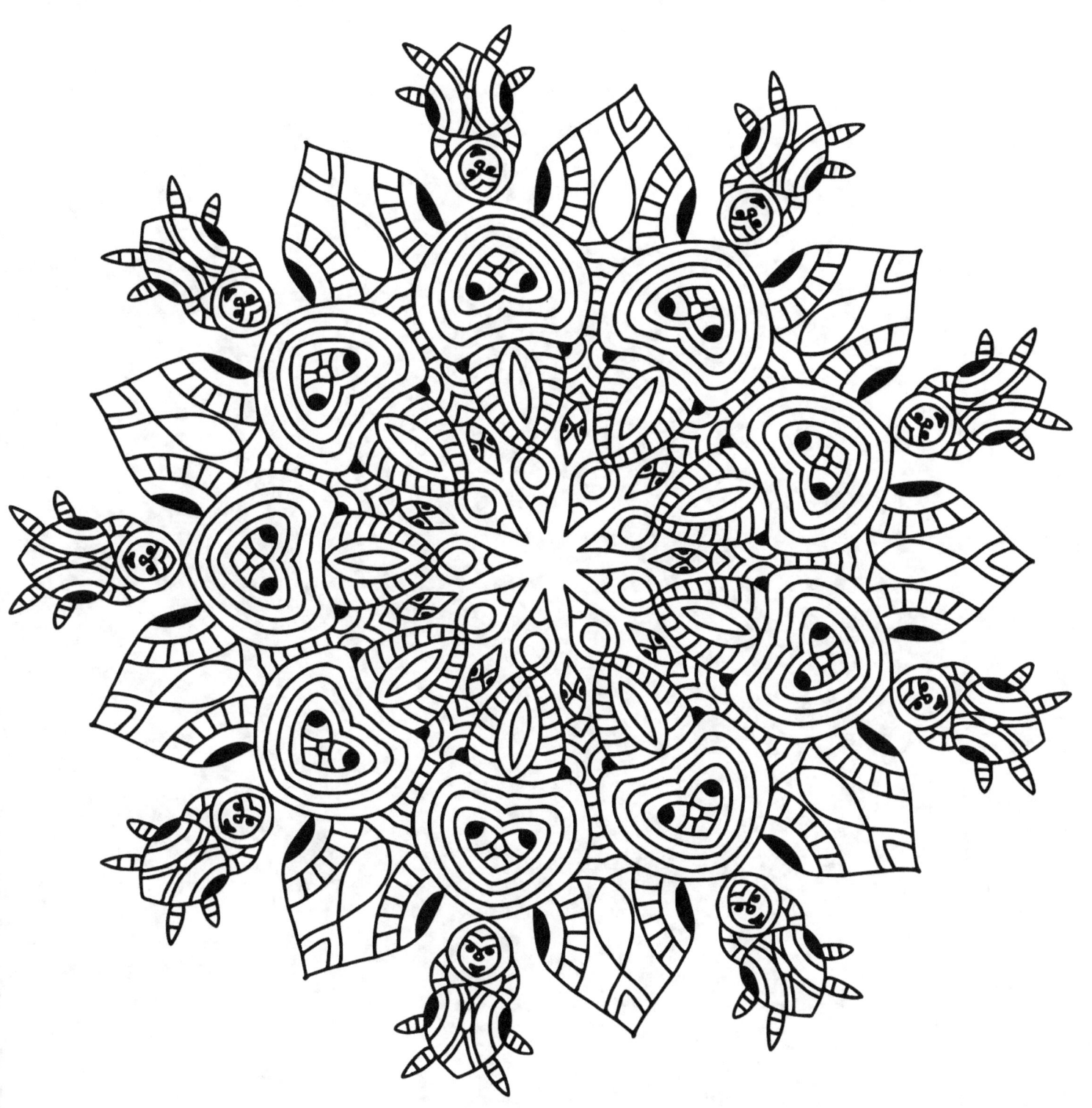

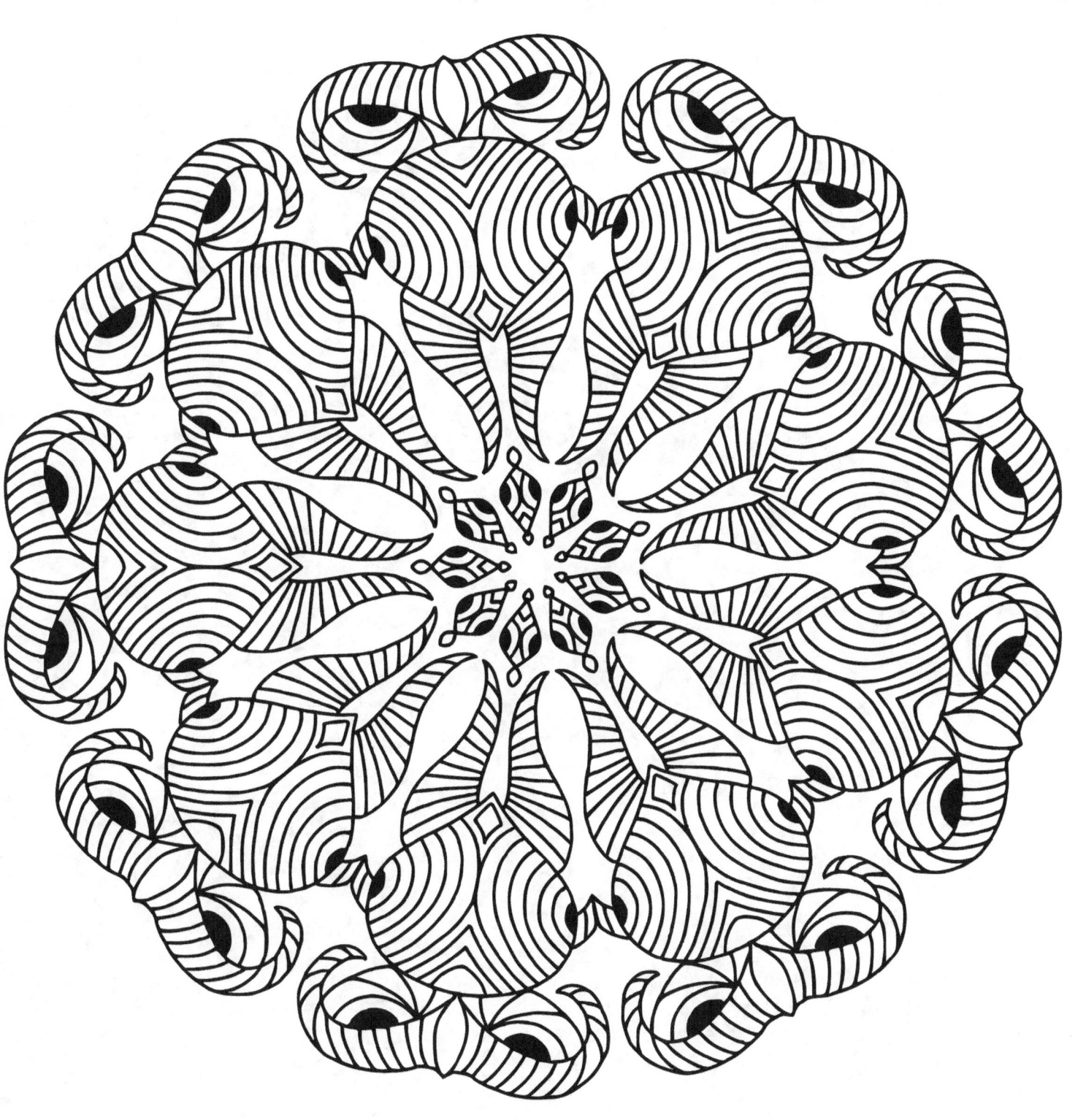

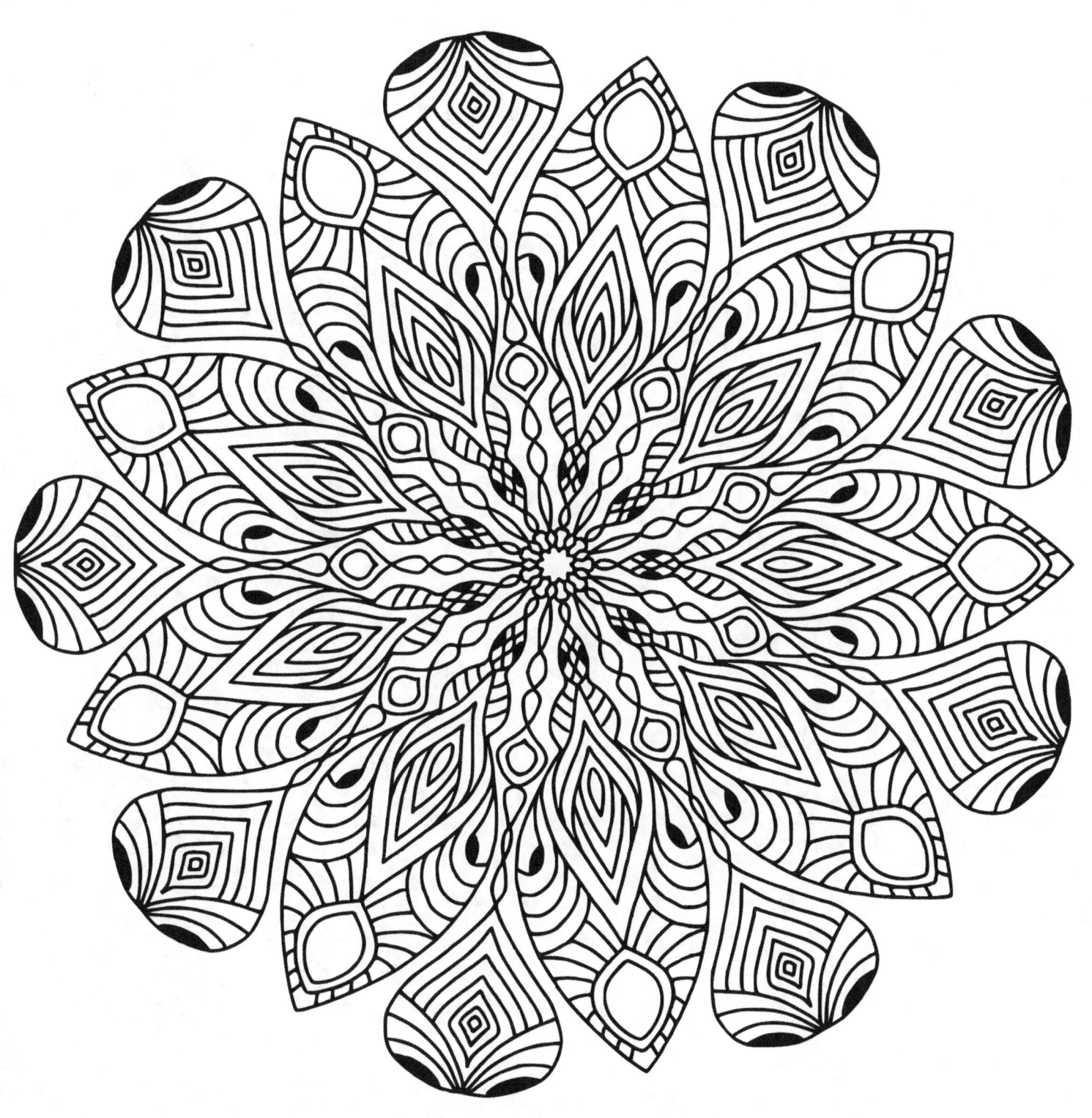

Test your colors here on the samples from
"My Pocket Coloring Companion"
&
"My Coloring Companion"

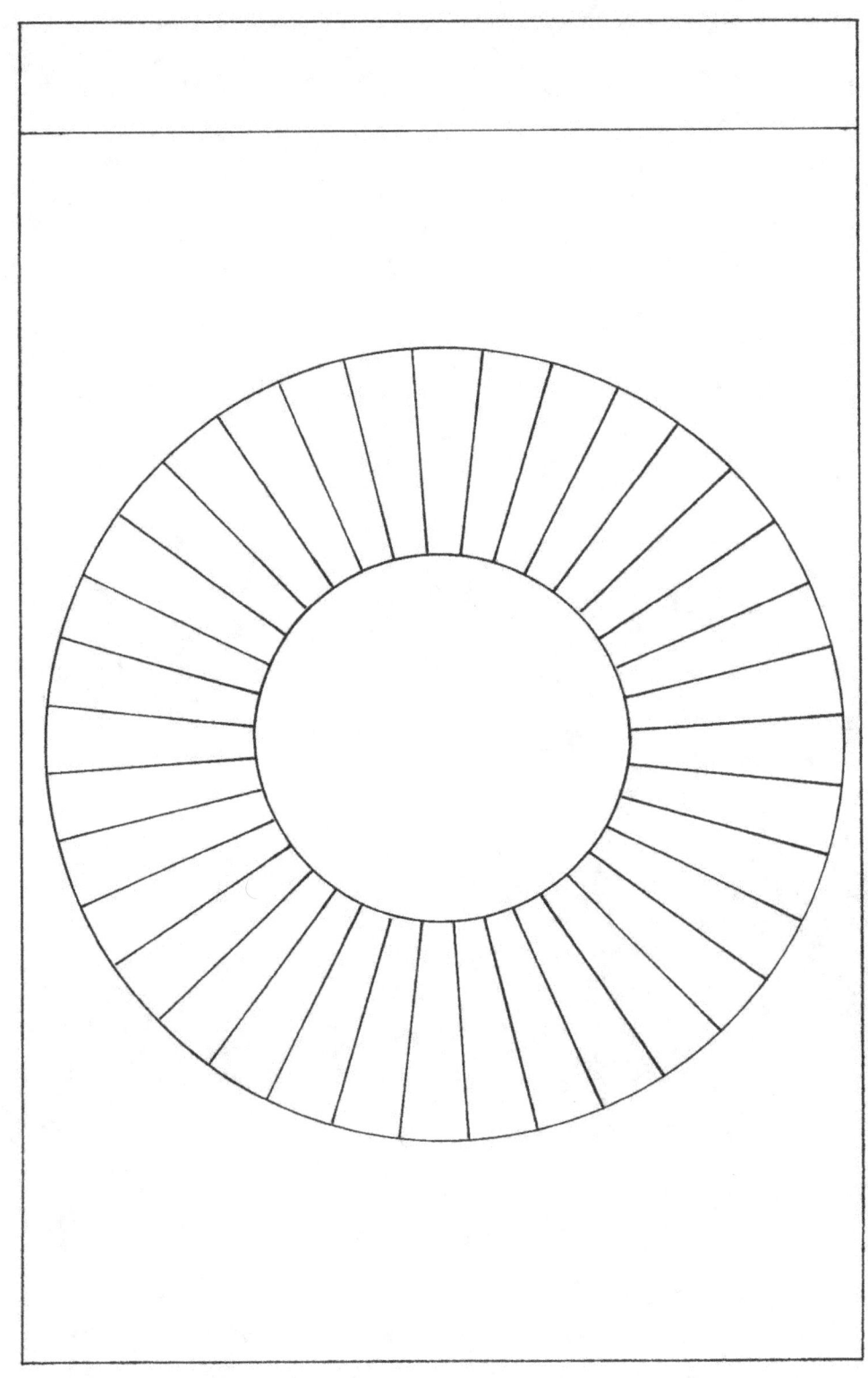

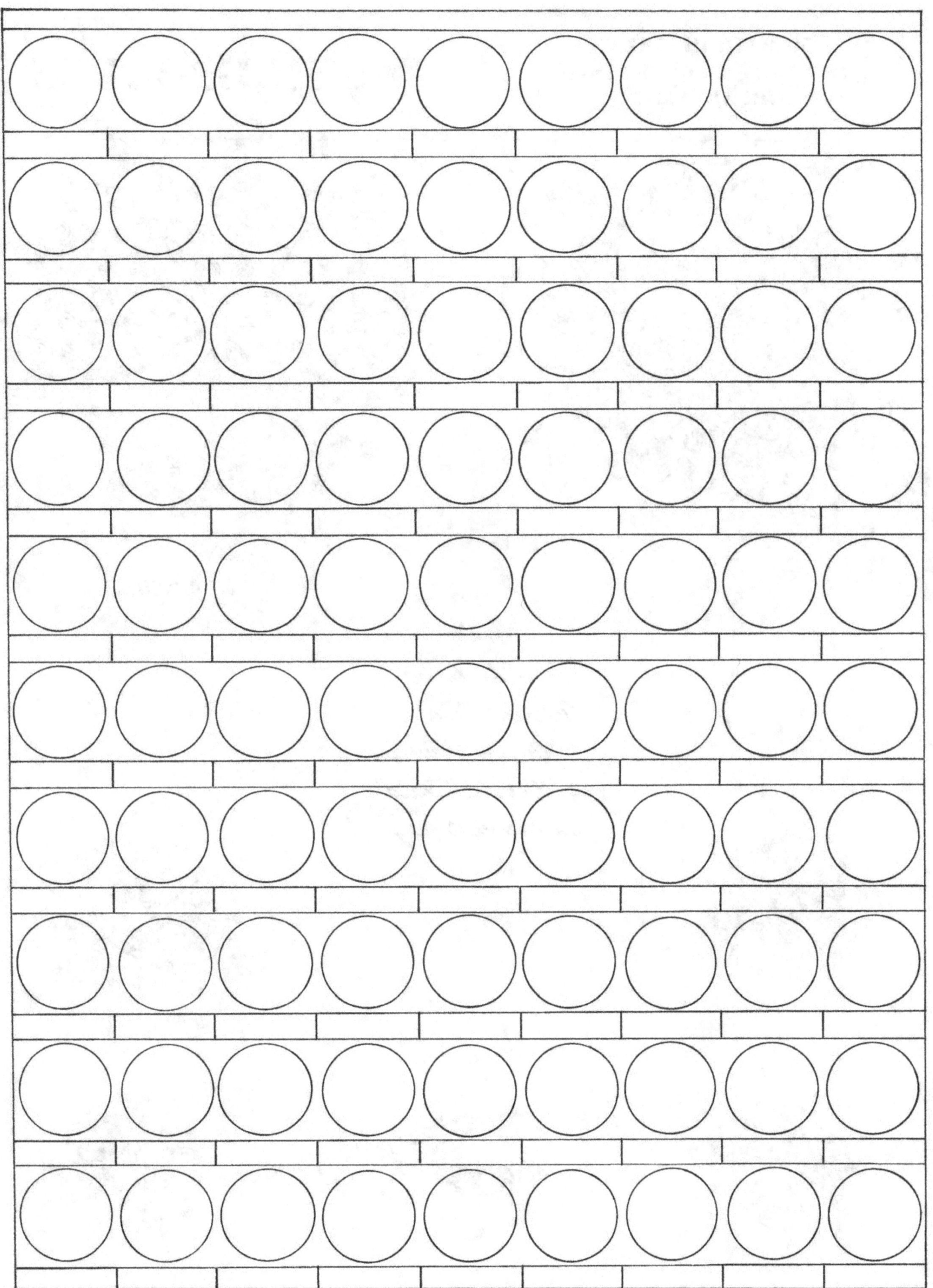

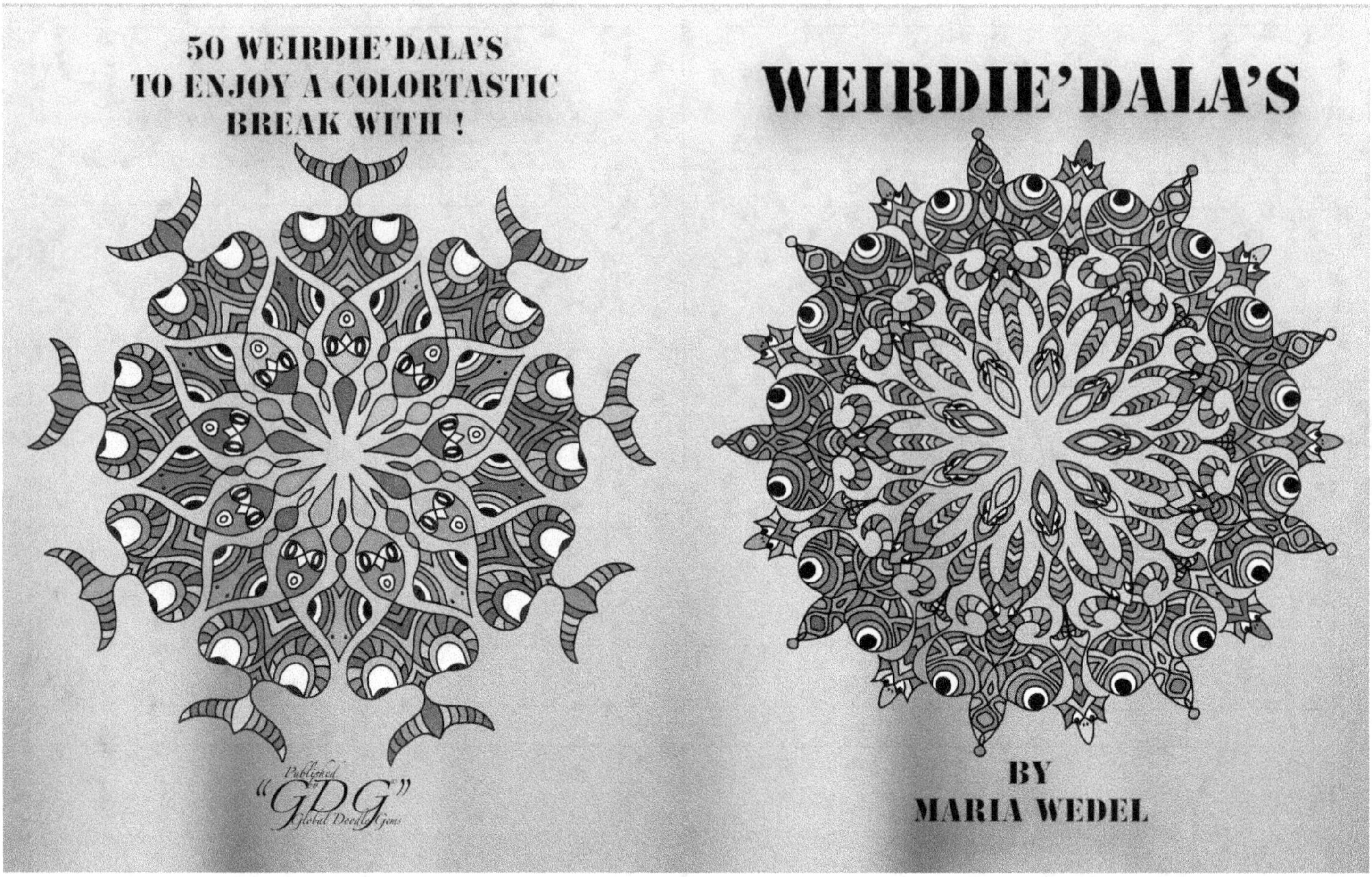

WEIRDIE'DALA'S

50 WEIRDIE'DALA'S TO ENJOY A COLORTASTIC BREAK WITH !

Published by "GDG" Global Doodle Gems

BY MARIA WEDEL

Check out Weirdie'Dala's 1 in the preview of Weirdie'Dala's 1 on the next pages !

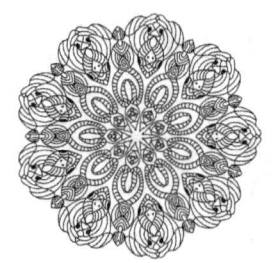
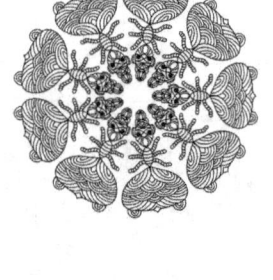
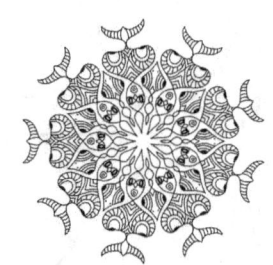
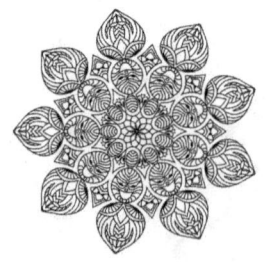
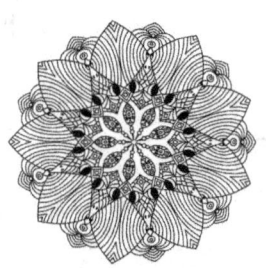

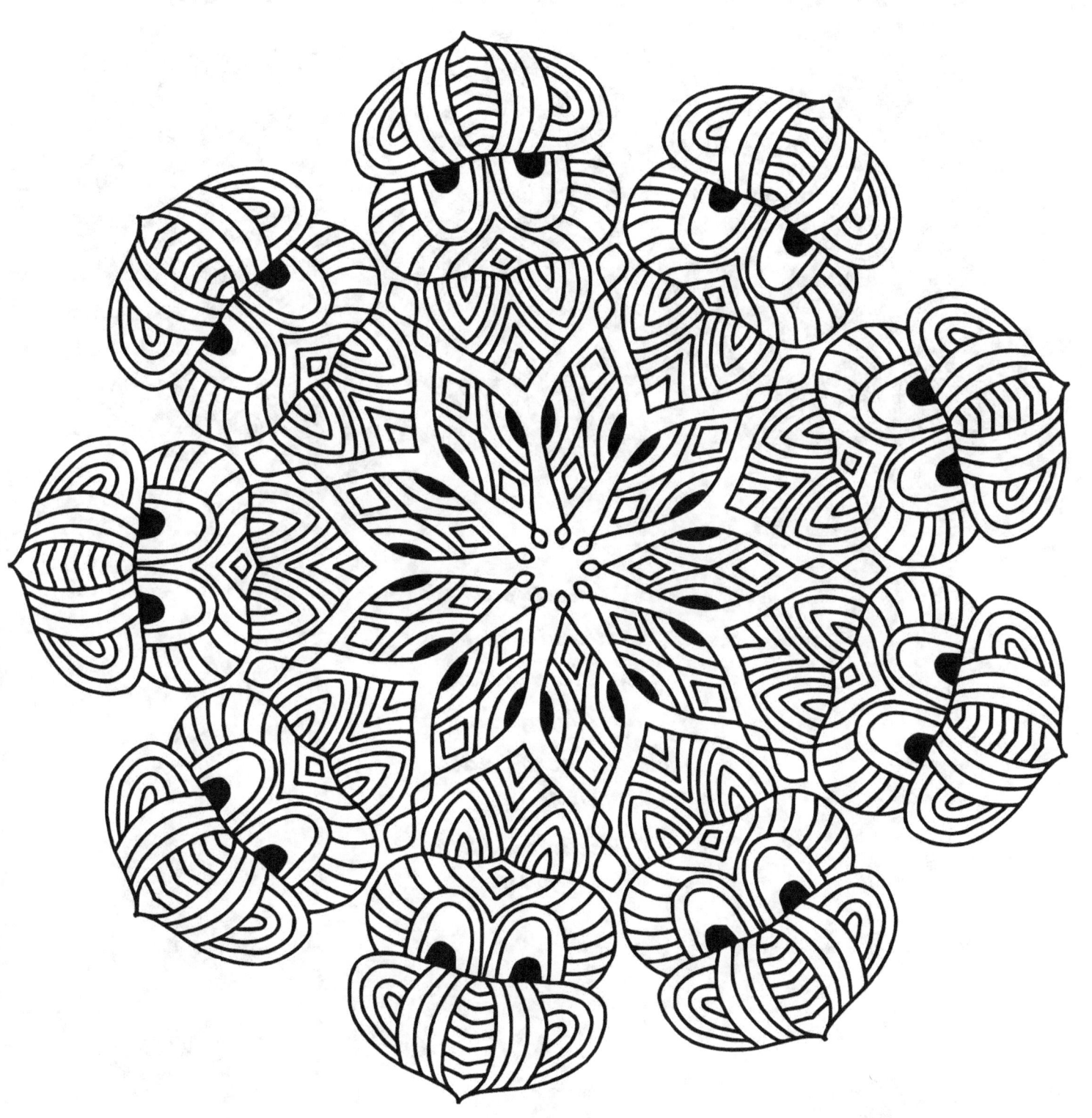

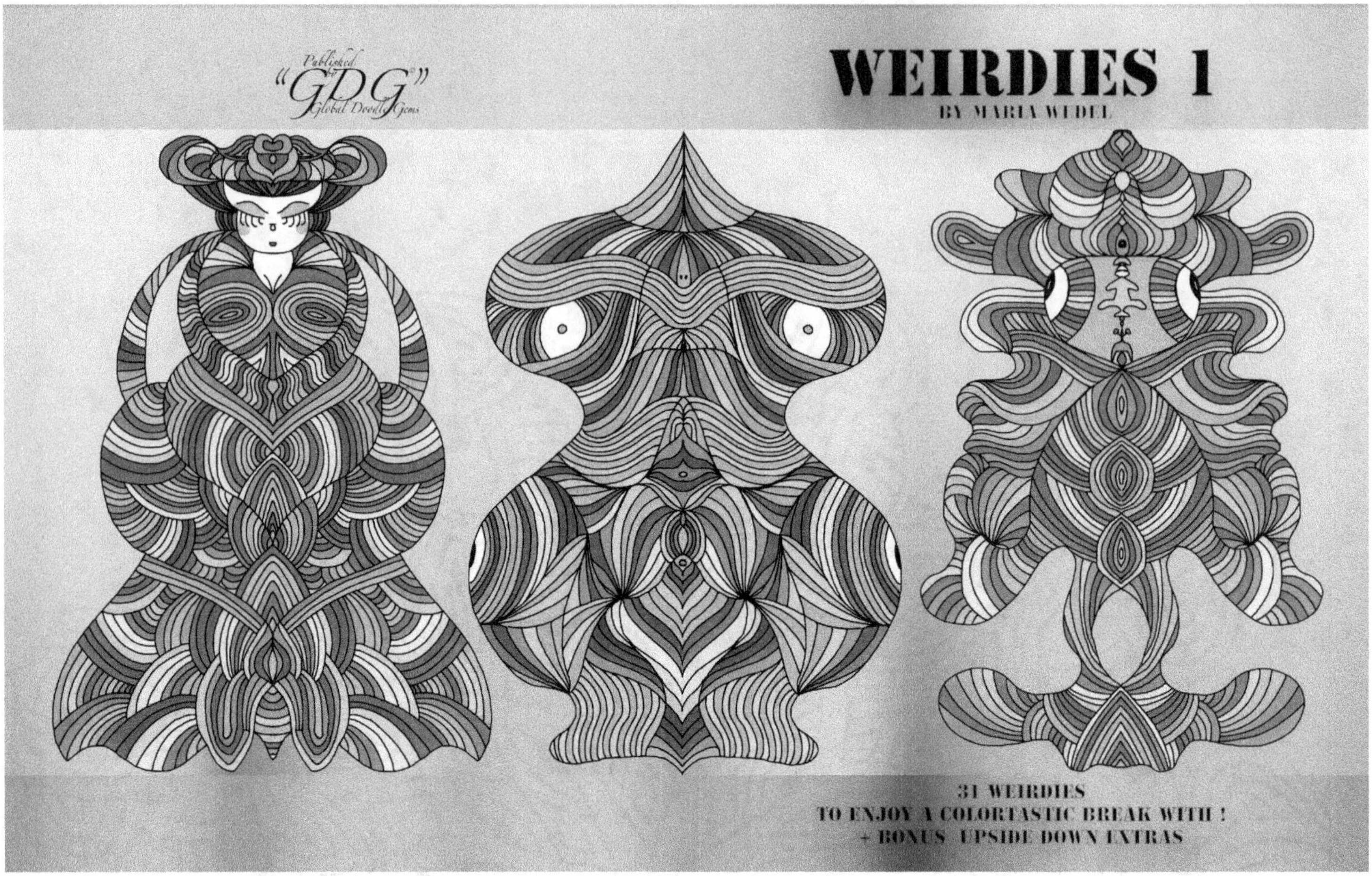

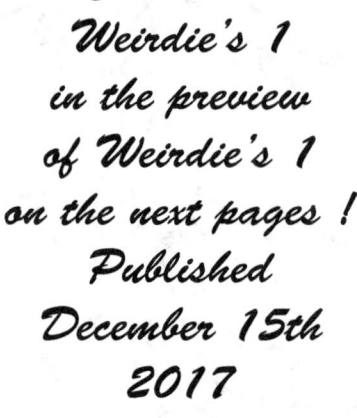

Check out
Weirdie's 1
in the preview
of Weirdie's 1
on the next pages !
Published
December 15th
2017

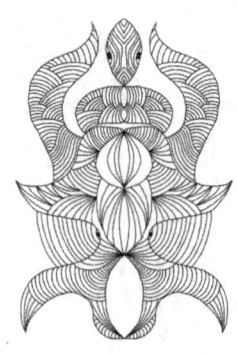
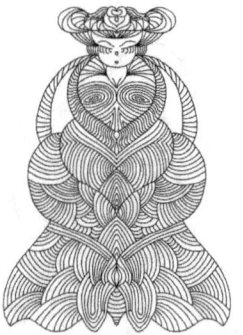
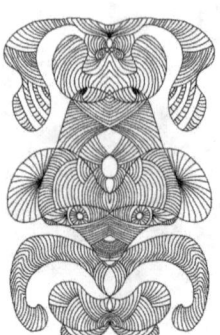
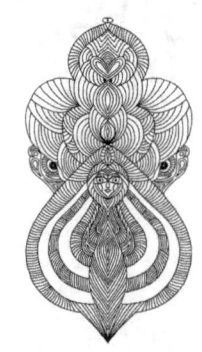
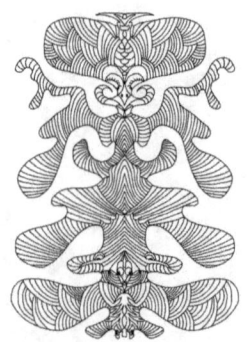

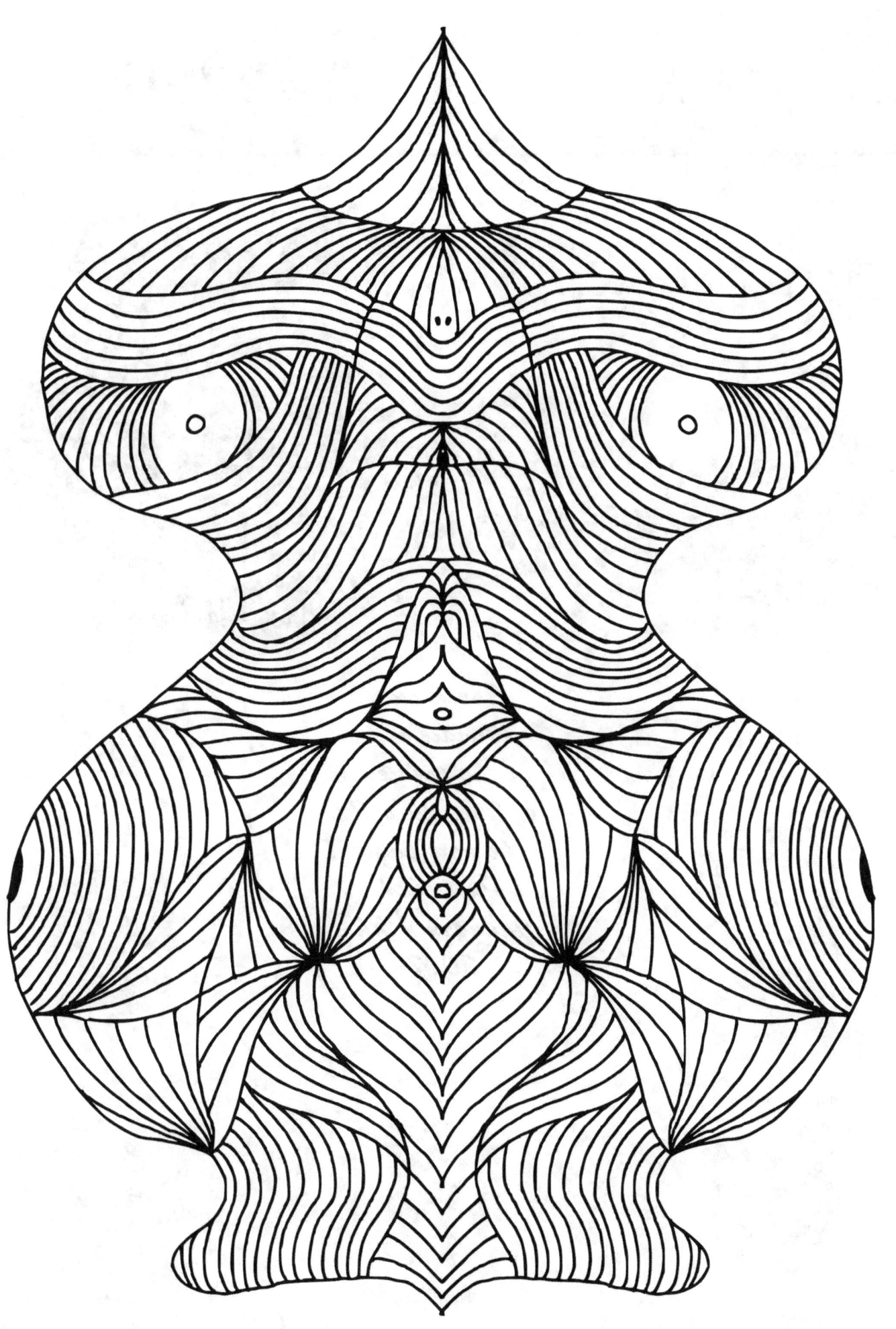

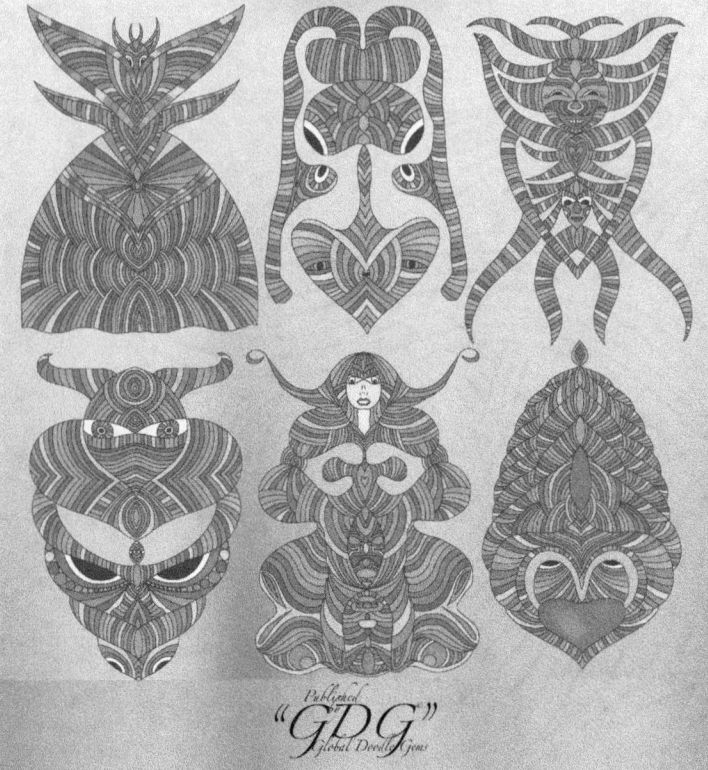
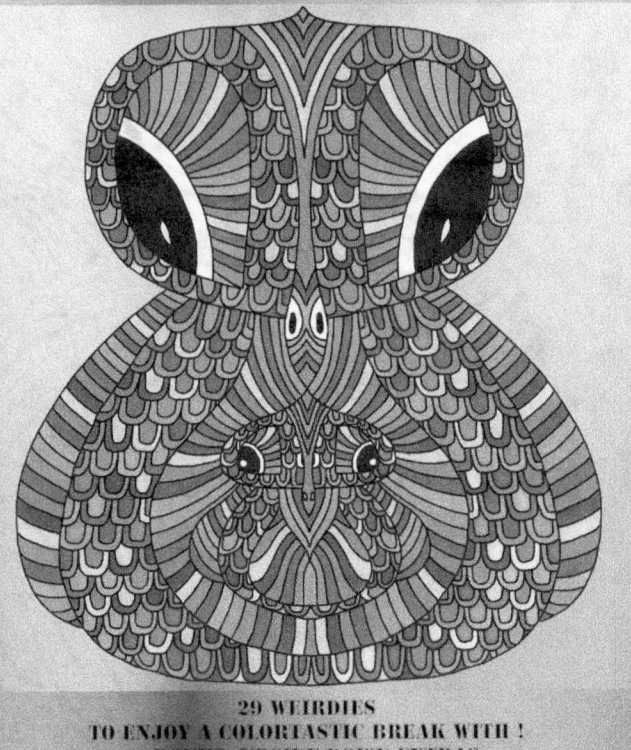

Check out
Weirdie's 2
in the preview
of Weirdie's 2
on the next pages !
Published
January 15th
2017

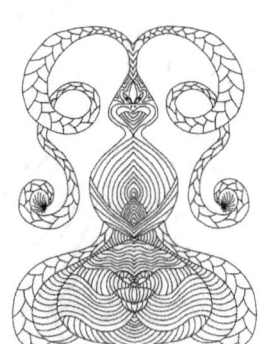
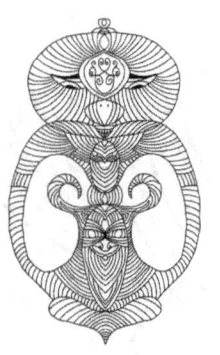
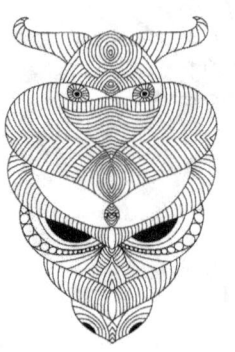
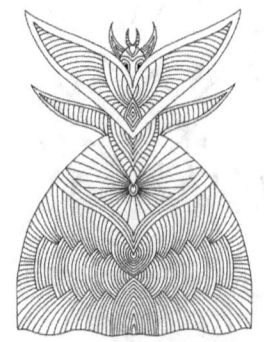
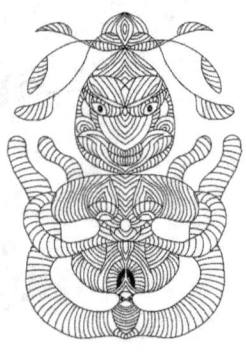

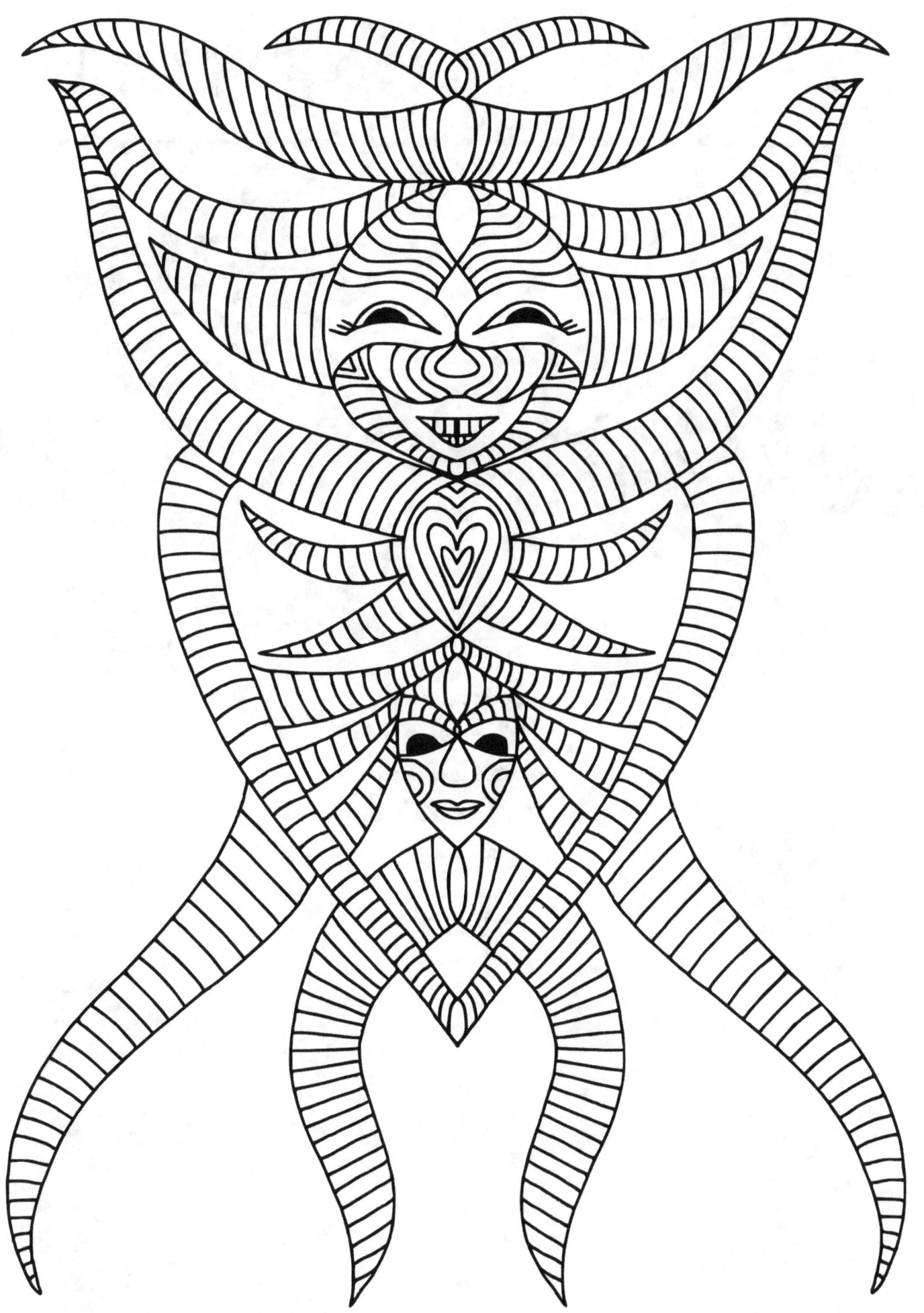

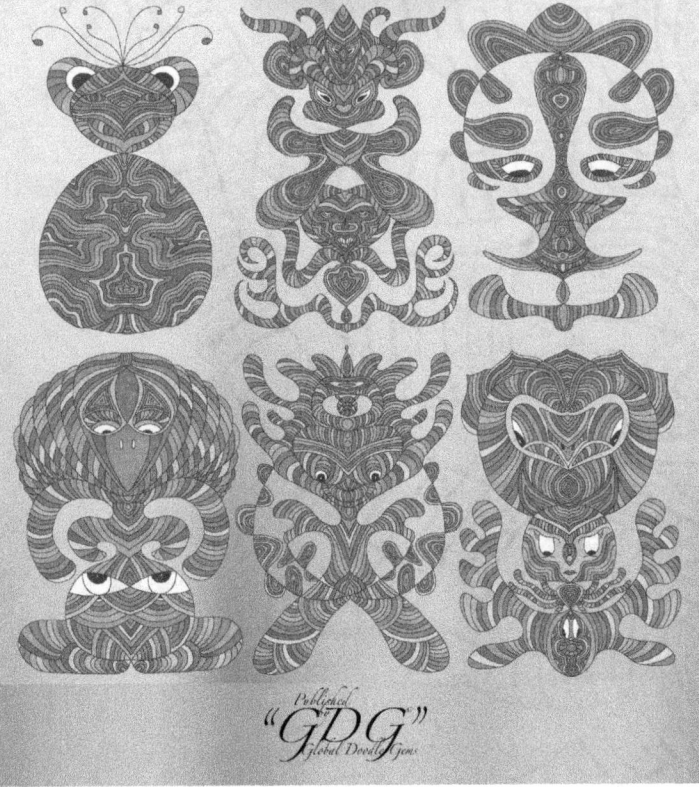
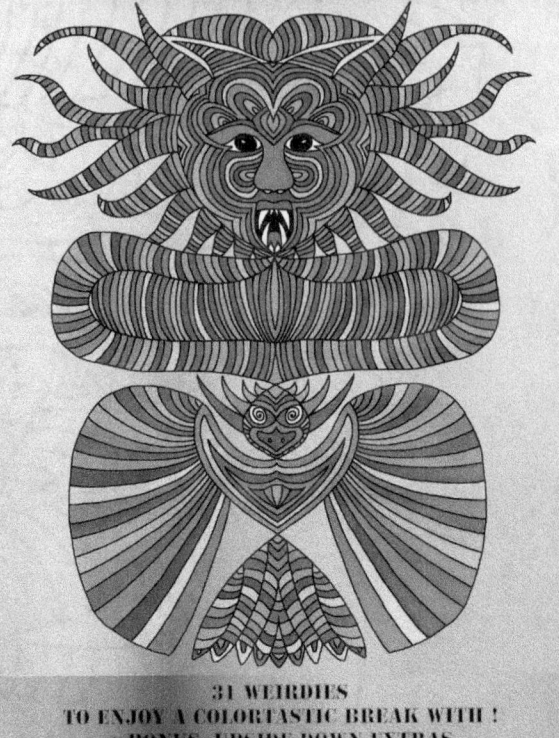

Check out
Weirdie's 3
in the preview
of Weirdie's 3
coming
Febuary 15th
2017

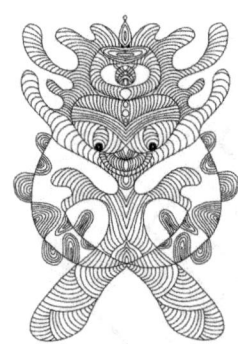
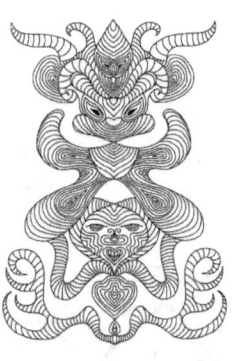
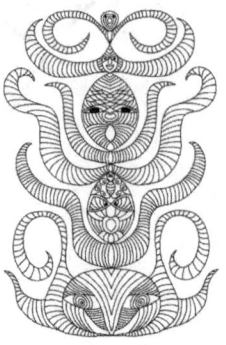
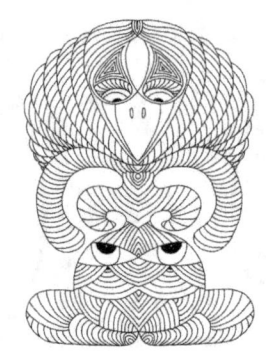
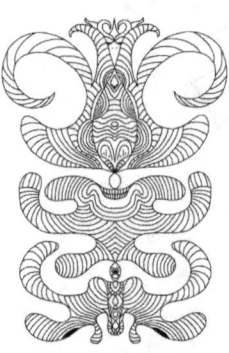

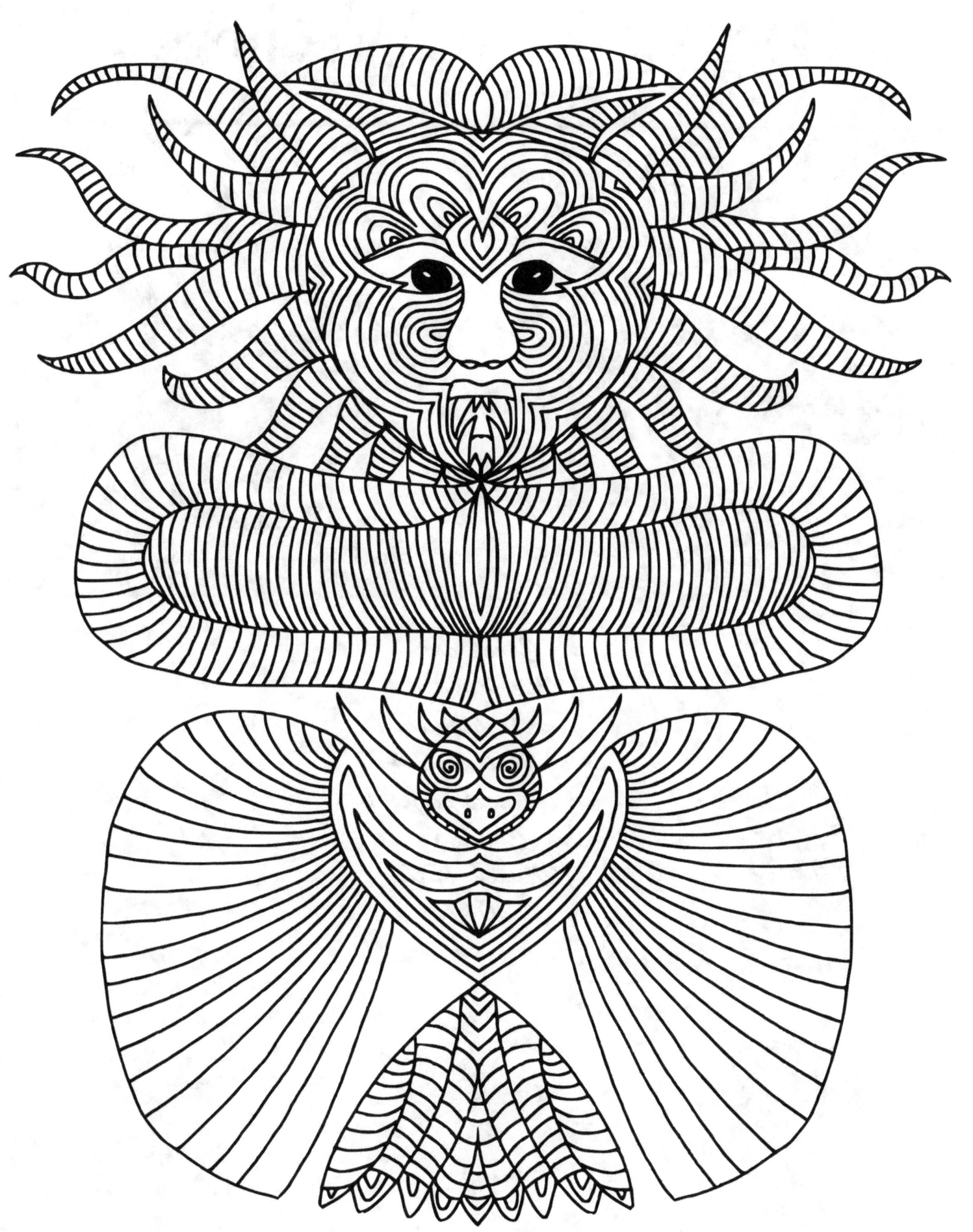

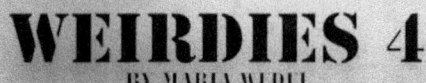
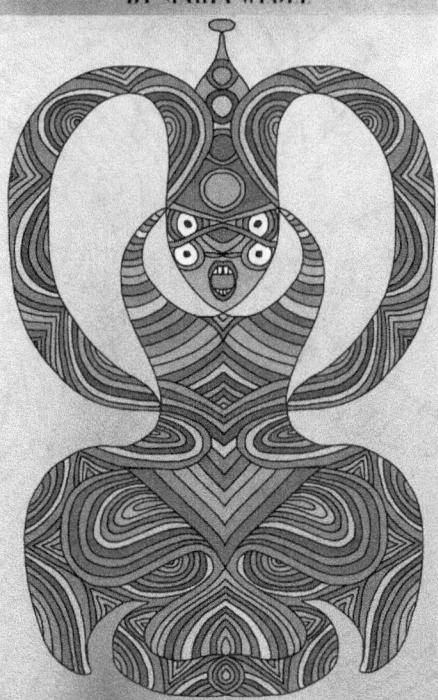
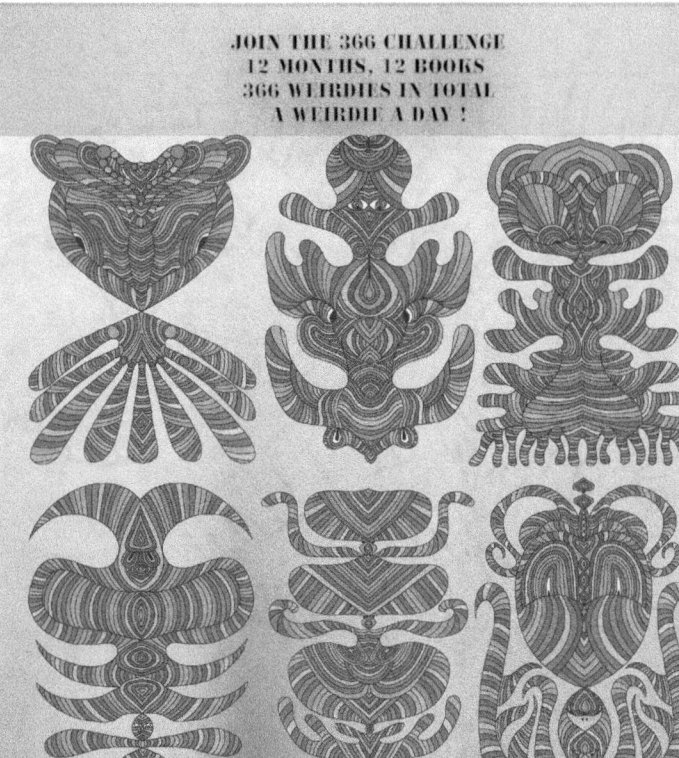

Check out Weirdie's 4 in the preview of Weirdie's 4 on the next pages! Coming March 15th 2017

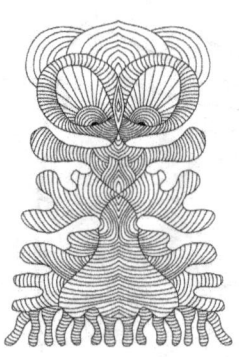
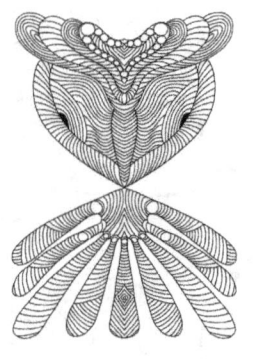
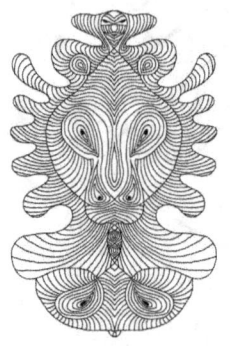
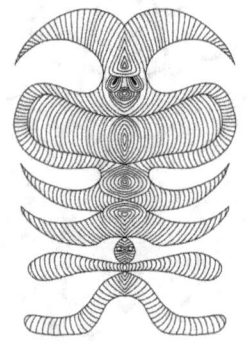
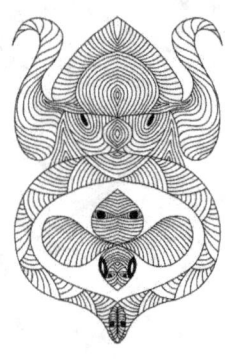

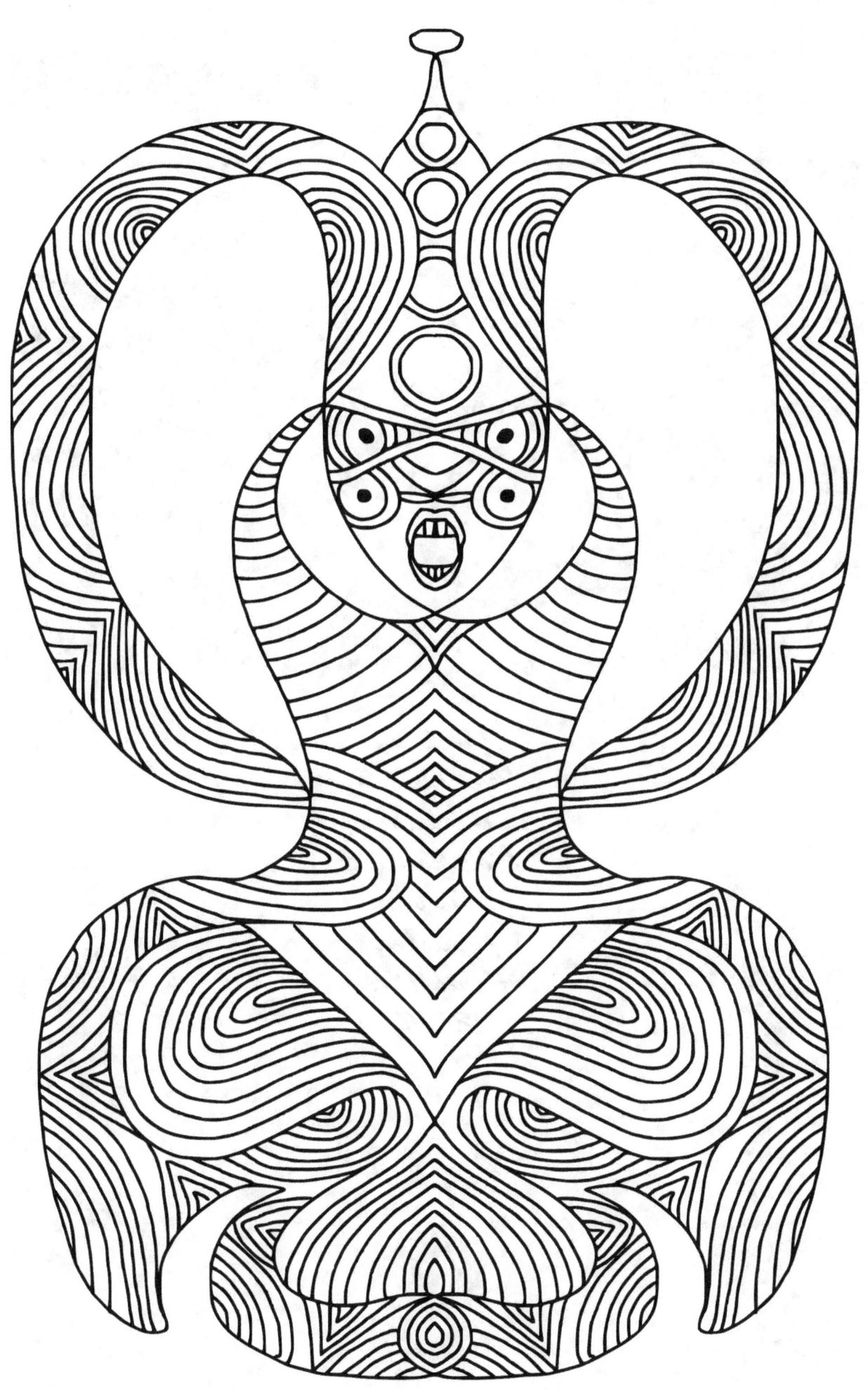

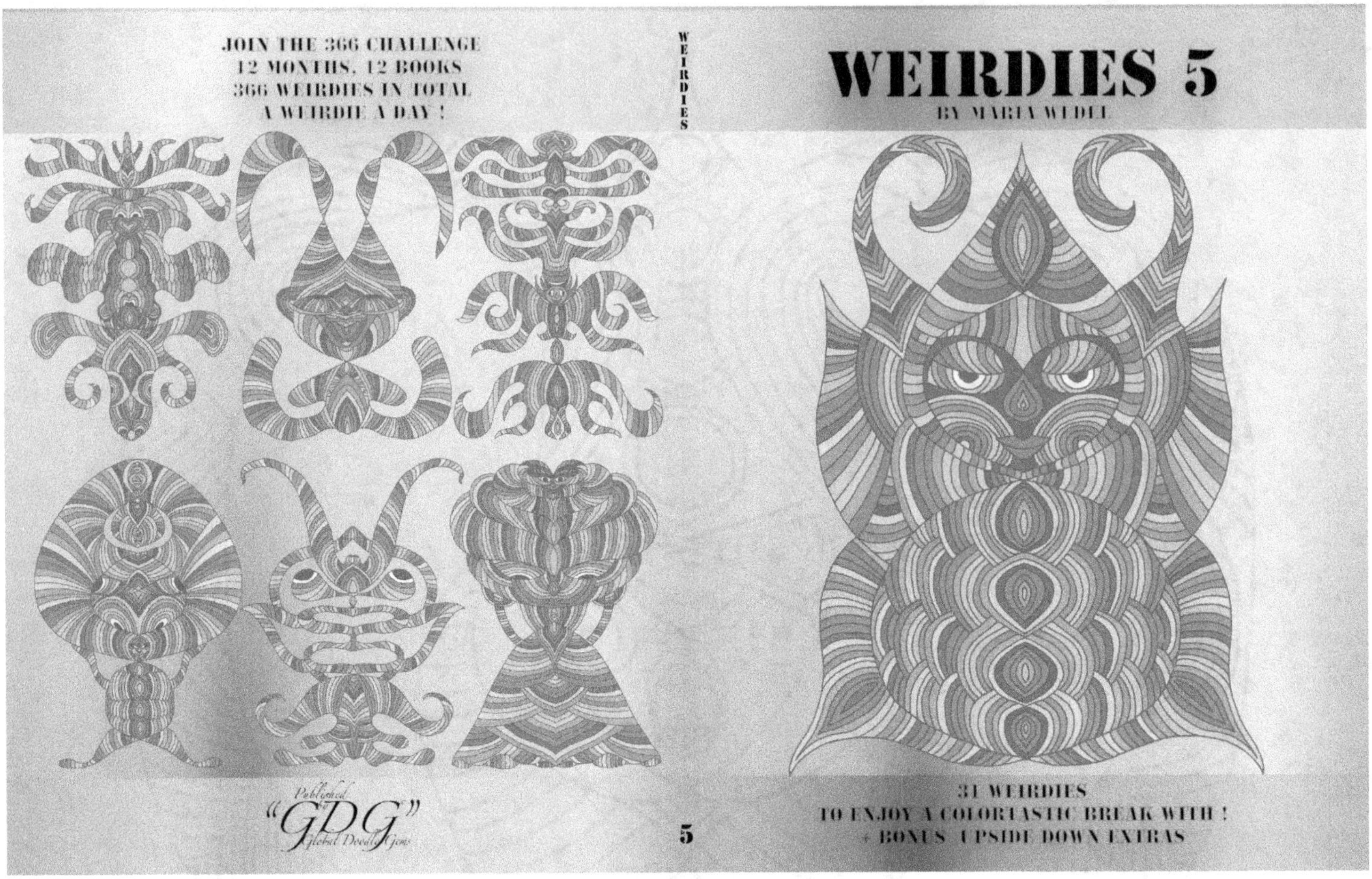

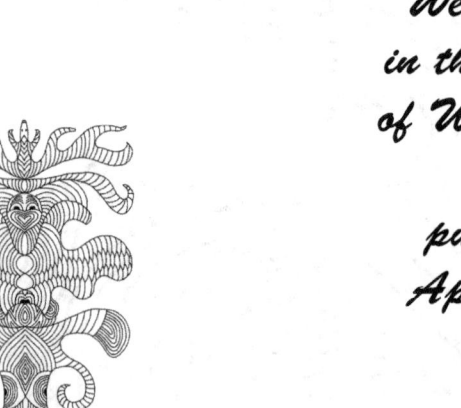

Check out
Weirdie's 5
in the preview
of Weirdie's 5
To be
published
April 15th
2017

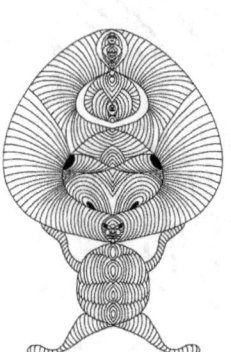
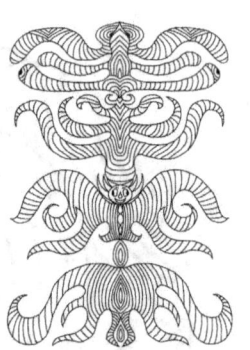
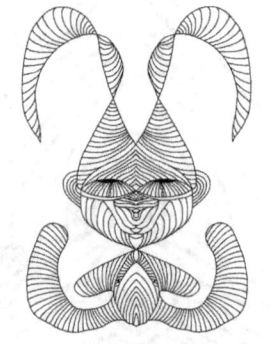
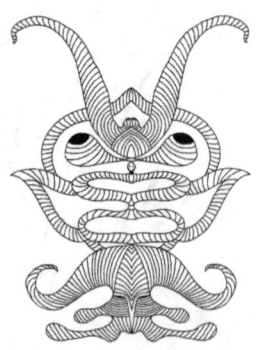

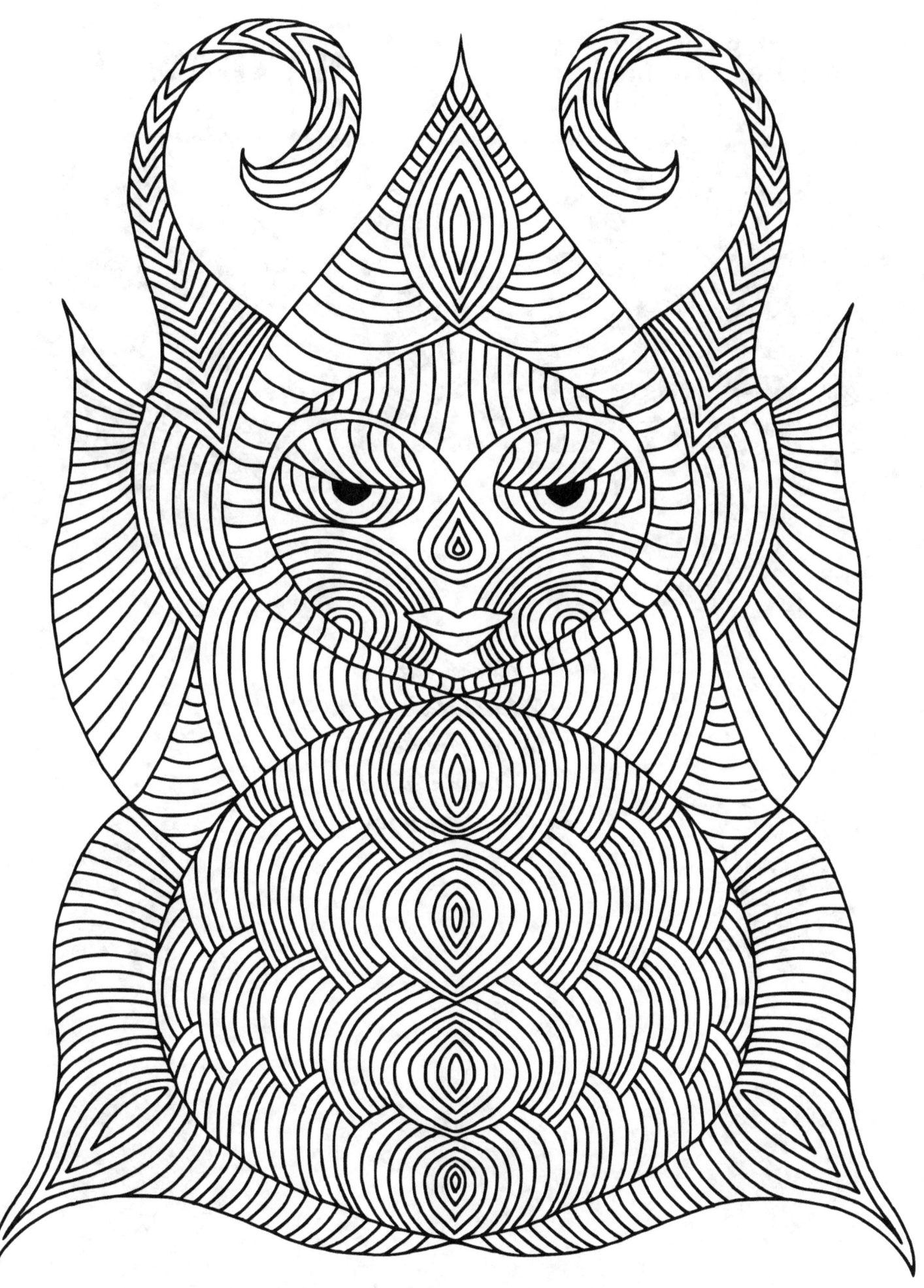

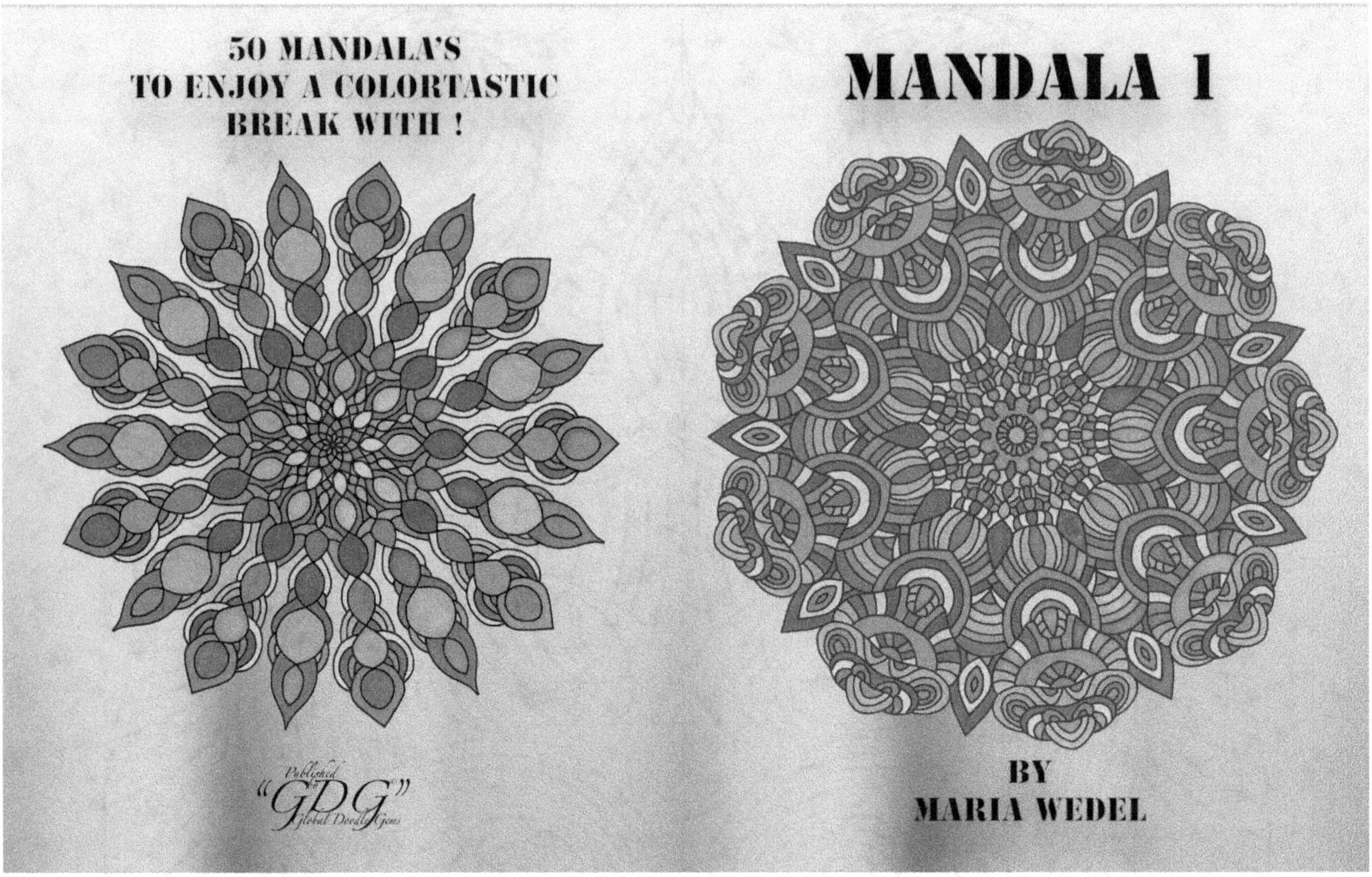

50 MANDALA'S TO ENJOY A COLORTASTIC BREAK WITH !

MANDALA 1

Published by "GDG" Global Doodle Gems

BY MARIA WEDEL

*Check out
Mandala's 1
in the preview
of Mandala's 1
on the next pages !*

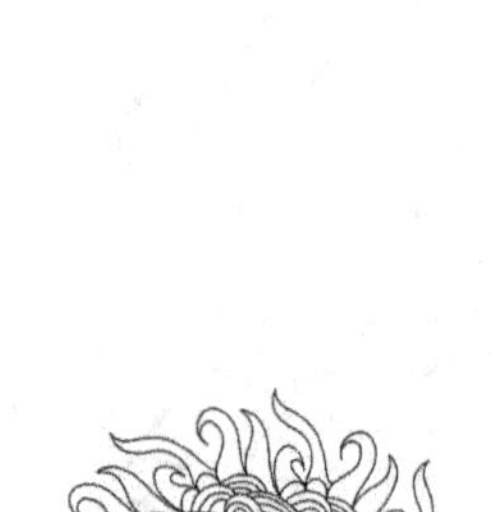

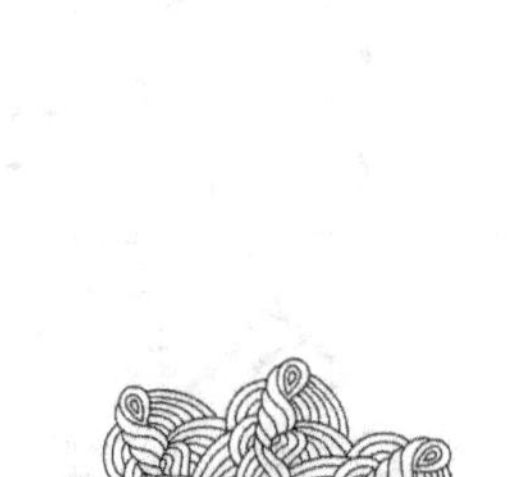

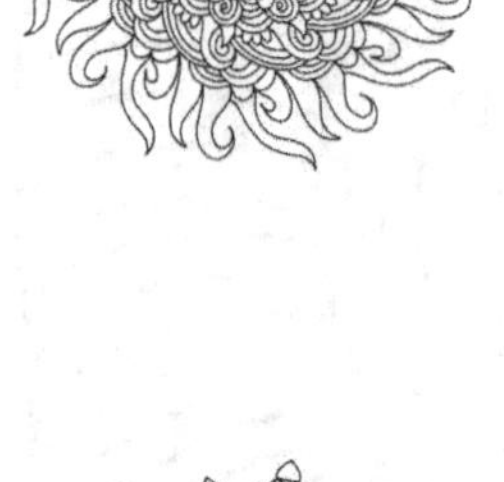

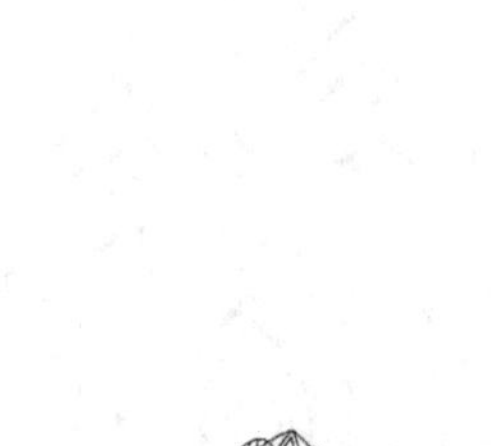

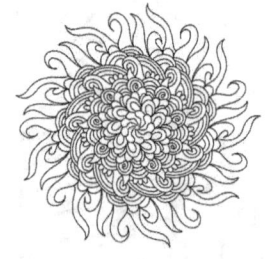
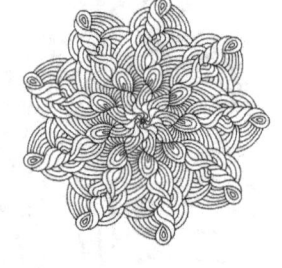
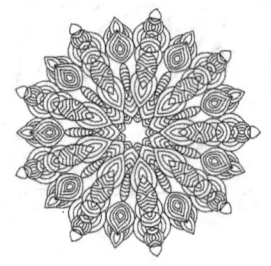
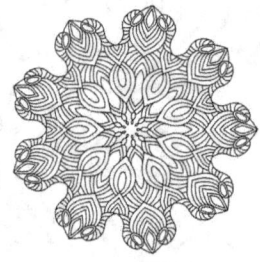
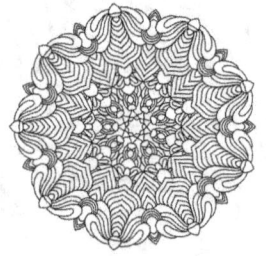

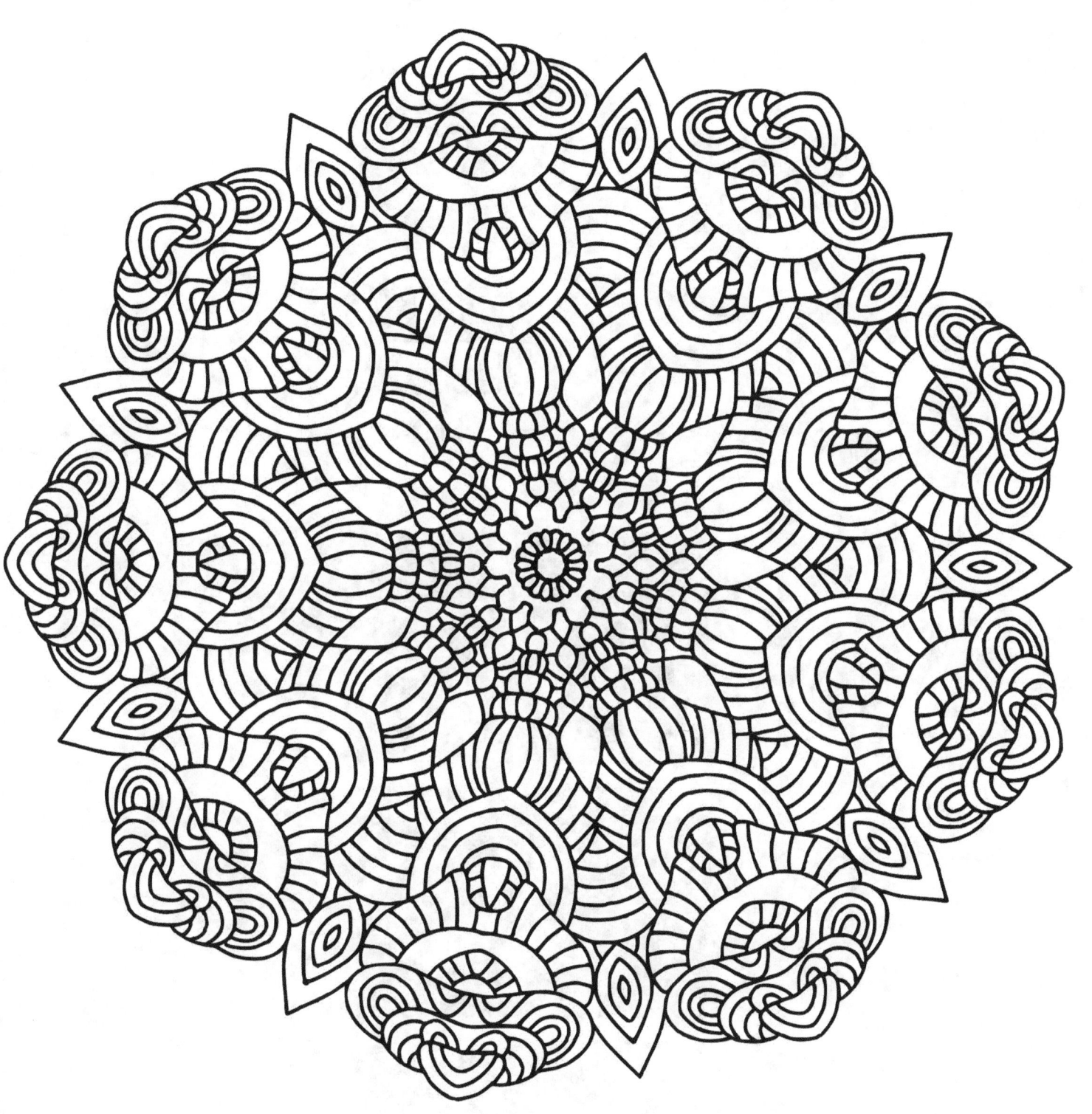

Other Titles by Maria Wedel

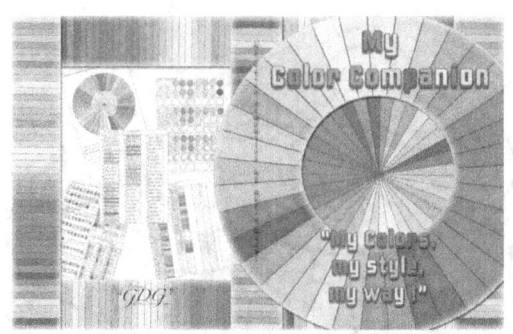

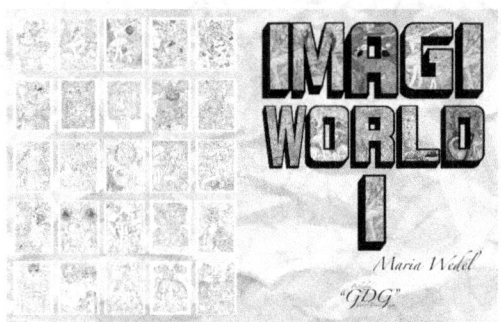

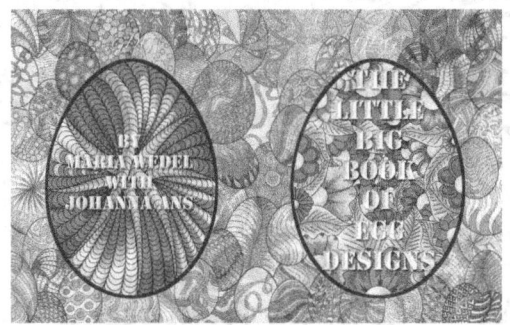

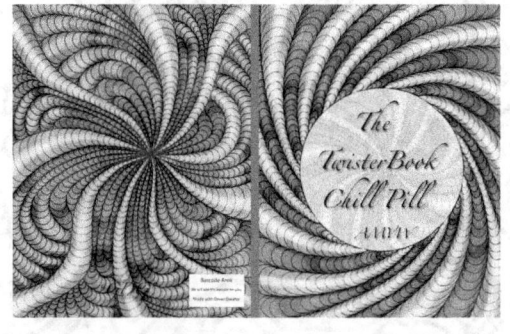

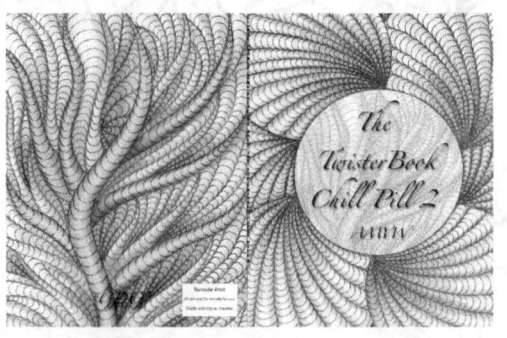

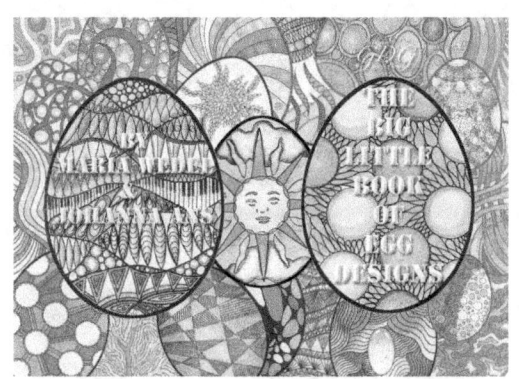
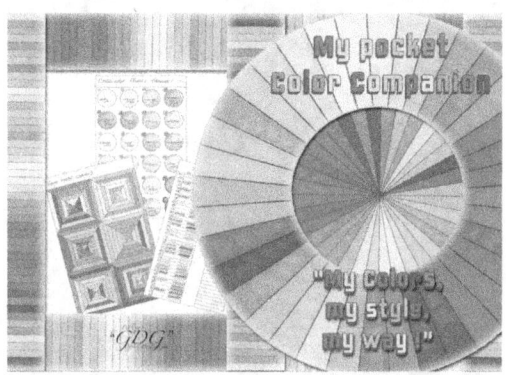
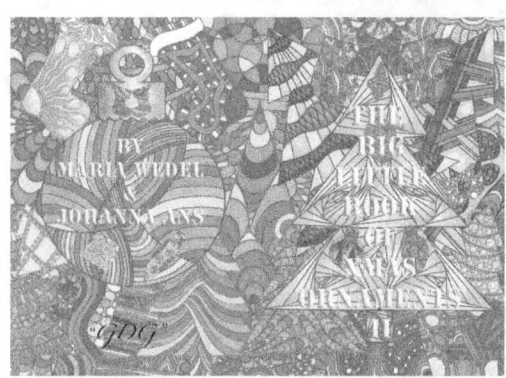
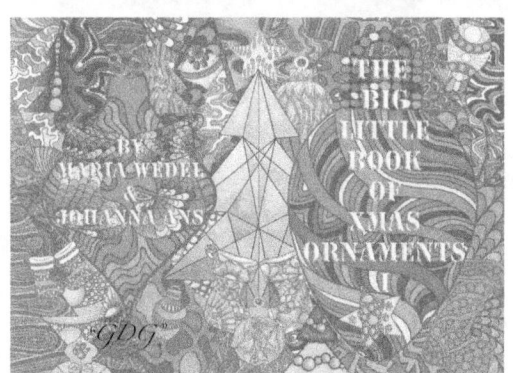
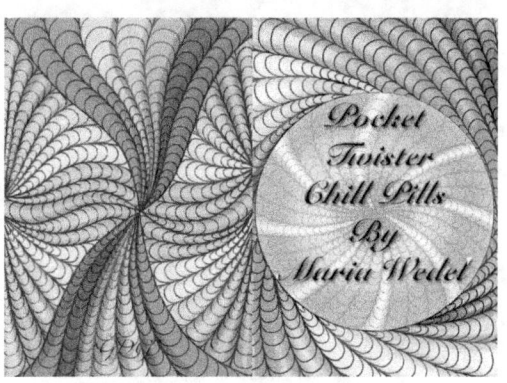

www.ingramcontent.com/pod-product-compliance
Lightning Source LLC
Chambersburg PA
CBHW082336220526
45470CB00008B/2537